BestMasters

Mit **„BestMasters“** zeichnet Springer die besten Masterarbeiten aus, die an renommierten Hochschulen in Deutschland, Österreich und der Schweiz entstanden sind. Die mit Höchstnote ausgezeichneten Arbeiten wurden durch Gutachter zur Veröffentlichung empfohlen und behandeln aktuelle Themen aus unterschiedlichen Fachgebieten der Naturwissenschaften, Psychologie, Technik und Wirtschaftswissenschaften. Die Reihe wendet sich an Praktiker und Wissenschaftler gleichermaßen und soll insbesondere auch Nachwuchswissenschaftlern Orientierung geben.

Springer awards **“BestMasters”** to the best master’s theses which have been completed at renowned Universities in Germany, Austria, and Switzerland. The studies received highest marks and were recommended for publication by supervisors. They address current issues from various fields of research in natural sciences, psychology, technology, and economics. The series addresses practitioners as well as scientists and, in particular, offers guidance for early stage researchers.

Christoph Wieser

Quantification of Structural Liquidity Risk in Banks

Springer Gabler

Christoph Wieser
Wien, Austria

Master Thesis, University of Applied Sciences BFI Vienna, Master's programme "Quantitative Asset and Risk Management", 2020

ISSN 2625-3577 ISSN 2625-3615 (electronic)
BestMasters
ISBN 978-3-658-39592-6 ISBN 978-3-658-39593-3 (eBook)
https://doi.org/10.1007/978-3-658-39593-3

Responsible Editor: Marija Kojic
This Springer Gabler imprint is published by the registered company Springer Fachmedien Wiesbaden GmbH, part of Springer Nature.
The registered company address is: Abraham-Lincoln-Str. 46, 65189 Wiesbaden, Germany

Abstract

Under Pillar 2 of the Basel Accords an assessment and quantification of all material risks is required. The corresponding process is called Internal Capital Adequacy Assessment Process (ICAAP) and it determines the amount of risk-bearing capacity the financial institution requires. Structural liquidity risk is a material risk resulting from the core banking business of taking in short-term deposits and lending out long-term loans, thus allowing a maturity mismatch between assets and liabilities. At some point the long-term loans will require refinancing and the institution is at risk of an adverse development of refinancing costs.

This thesis proposes a model for the quantification of structural liquidity risk. The institution's credit spread is identified as sole source of risk and its future development is modelled using Monte Carlo simulation. The underlying process of the credit spread evolution is a jump-diffusion process. The 99.9% quantile of the simulated distribution of terminal values is added on top of the swap rates to represent the stressed refinancing costs. The change in present value between closing open liquidity positions under stressed refinancing costs compared to current costs is the calculated impact on risk-bearing capacity.

The proposed model provides the basis for a more sophisticated model to quantify structural liquidity risk by mitigating identified weaknesses and implementing suggested improvements.

Contents

Abbreviations

ALCO	Asset-Liability Committee
ALMM	Additional Liquidity Monitoring Metrics
ASF	Available Stable Funding
bAJD	basic Affine Jump-Diffusion model
BCBS	Basel Committee on Banking Supervision
CB	Central Bank
CBC	Counterbalancing Capacity
CDF	Cumulative Distribution Function
CDS	Credit Default Swap
CF	Cashflow
CFP	Contingency Funding Plan
CIR	Cox-Ingersoll-Ross
CKLS	Chan-Karolyi-Longstaff-Sanders
CPR	Constant Prepayment Rate
CRD	Capital Requirements Directive
CRR	Capital Requirements Regulation
EBA	European Banking Agency
EC	Economic Capital
EL	Expected Loss
EWI	Early Warning Indicator
FI	Financial Institution
FMA	Financial Market Authority
HQLA	High-Quality Liquid Assets
ICAAP	Internal Capital Adequacy Assessment Process
ILAAP	Internal Liquidity Adequacy Assessment Process
ITS	Implementing Technical Standards

LaR	Liquidity at Risk
LCR	Liquidity Coverage Ratio
LVaR	Liquidity Value at Risk
NSFR	Net Stable Funding Ratio
OAS	Option-Adjusted Spread
OU	Ornstein-Uhlenbeck
PMF	Probability Mass Function
PnL	Profit and Loss
PV	Present Value
RSF	Required Stable Funding
SDE	Stochastic Differential Equation
S&P	Standard & Poor's
SREP	Supervisory Review and Evaluation Process
UL	Unexpected Loss
VaR	Value at Risk
VLaR	Value Liquidity at Risk

List of Figures

List of Tables

1 Introduction

Structural liquidity risk describes the risk emerging from follow-up financing, also referred to as funding liquidity risk, liquidity cost risk, liquidity spread risk or liquidity maturity transformation risk. This risk is the result of a maturity mismatch of assets and liabilities. This mismatch arises from the bank's core business activities of taking in short-term deposits and lending out long-term loans.[1]

The difference to liquidity risk in the short-term perspective (measured by the Liquidity Coverage Ratio) is that structural liquidity risk is a long-term factor. This type of liquidity risk refers to the fact that the cost of liquidity for the purpose of closing liquidity gaps[2] can change if refinancing becomes more expensive, for instance due to a decline in the bank's creditworthiness. If the bank's credit quality deteriorates, refinancing can become more expensive regardless of interest levels. This can be observed in the expansion of credit spreads on the money and capital markets. In such cases, a bank will have to pay more for refinancing in the future due to the decline in its creditworthiness.

Conceptually, the risk can be calculated by assuming a rating migration and the resulting effects on credit spreads. The risk capital need results from the present-value cost difference between refinancing on current terms and refinancing (for example) after a simulated rating migration.

Structural liquidity risk is especially significant when a bank refinances to a great extent on the money and capital markets, or with other banks.[3]

---

[1] Ruozi/Ferrari (2013) p. 8

[2] A gap is the difference between maturing assets (inflows) and maturing liabilities (outflows) in a specified time bucket.

[3] Thonabauer/Nösslinger (2006) p. 50

C. Wieser, *Quantification of Structural Liquidity Risk in Banks*, BestMasters,
https://doi.org/10.1007/978-3-658-39593-3_1

The quantification of the structural liquidity risk is part of the Internal Capital Adequacy and Assessment Process (ICAAP) as it is deemed a significant risk arising from banking transactions and banking operations. The ICAAP is based on adequate risk management, which ensures that the risks to which the credit institution is exposed, are identified, measured, reported and controlled.[4]

The topic is highly relevant to credit institutions because an appropriate model is required. The models used by the banks are tailored internal solutions and undisclosed information.

There are currently no papers or books that discuss different approaches or models that are able to fulfill the ICAAP requirements, but methodological frameworks for the quantification of structural liquidity risk can be found in Matz et. al. (2007), Bartetzky et al. (2008) and Enthofer/Haas (2018).

1.1 Research Question

How to quantify a bank's structural liquidity risk?

The result of the quantification is a figure that shows which amount of economic capital must be held to mitigate the risk of higher refinancing costs. This figure represents a loss that could result from increased funding costs:

What is the maximum loss in present value at a certain confidence level (99.9%) over a specified period (1 year or 250 trading days)?

The goal of this thesis is to provide a model that produces the figure mentioned above.

1.2 General Approach and Methodology

This subsection states the topics introduced within the subsequent chapters, as well as the research methods and provides an overview of the most important sources of information.

Chapter 2 introduces the concept of liquidity and its risk. There are several possible subcategorizations of liquidity risk to be found in the literature. But a common understanding of the importance of the timeframe may be observed. Bartetzky et al. (2008), the Basel Committee on Banking Supervision (2008), Duttweiler (2009), Ruozi/Ferrari (2013) and Schierenbeck (2008) provide the literary basis for this chapter. Especially the book "Handbuch Liquiditätsrisiko" by

[4] Financial Market Authority (2020) n.pag.

Dr. Peter Bartetzky, who is managing director of a consulting company specialized on treasury topics, provides valuable inputs that are not only limited to this chapter.

Liquidity risk regulation and what it requires from liquidity risk management is listed with details in Chapter 3. The liquidity coverage ratio (LCR), the net stable funding ratio (NSFR), as well as other templates for regulatory reporting (additional monitoring metrics) comprise important regulatory topics, but of special relevance to this thesis is Subsection 3.4 about ICAAP and the concept of economic capital.

Publications of the Basel Committee on Banking Supervision (2013, 2014), the European Banking Authority (2014) and Venkat/Baird (2013) are major information sources in the first 3 subsections. For the details on ICAAP and economic capital the respective subsection refers to Enthofer/Haas (2018), Thonabauer/Nösslinger (2006) and Porteous/Tapadar (2006).

Shyam Venkat and Stephen Baird are risk professionals currently employed at PricewaterhouseCoopers (PwC). Their book provides well reflected background information that BCBS and EBA publications on liquidity risk regulation lack. Hannes Enthofer and Patrick Haas deliver within their book on asset liability management important ideas and measures not just contributing to the subsection on ICAAP.

Chapter 4 describes the tools and models used in the daily business of liquidity risk managers. The foundation for creating a liquidity balance sheet is built, which provides the most critical input parameters, namely liquidity gaps to the proposed model in Chapter 5. The computation of a liquidity balance sheet heavily relies on models for non-deterministic cashflows. The main approaches for the modelling of sight deposits, prepayments and credit lines are listed with a limited grade of detail.

Subsection 4.1 on the liquidity balance sheet is based on literature research of Bartetzky et al. (2008), Schmaltz (2009), Castagna/Fede (2013), Schultz (2016), Duttweiler (2009) and Enthofer/Haas (2018).

Antonio Castagna and Francesco Fede are experts in the field of derivative pricing. Their book on measuring and managing liquidity risk contributes a lot to this subsection, as it provides a well-balanced overview on modelling stochastic cashflows of various product types.

Stress testing, intraday liquidity risk management, early warning indicators and contingency planning are other major subsections within Chapter 4. Some additional sources, that have not been mentioned for this section so far, are utilized: Matz et al. (2007), Venkat/Baird (2013) and Basel Committee on Banking Supervision (2013).

Leonard Matz is a US-based banking expert who has also published books on interest rate risk and asset-liability management. His practitioner's guide on liquidity risk management vividly reflects the concepts of stress testing and contingency planning.

Chapter 4 closes with a subsection on stochastic model concepts. The liquidity value at risk approach is of particular importance to this thesis, as the underlying idea is the same as in the proposed model in Chapter 5. Deutsche Bundesbank (2008) and Bartetzky et al. (2008) provide the literary basis for this subsection.

Chapter 5 introduces the concepts, tools and models used for the quantification of structural liquidity risk. The framework used is adopted from Enthofer/Haas (2018) and referred to as liquidity cost risk. Hannes Enthofer and Patrick Haas embedded their concept of liquidity cost risk into the regulatory scenarios of ICAAP.

The implementation of a jump-diffusion model for stressing the risk factor is original to this thesis. A Monte Carlo method is used to simulate numerous trajectories of the risk factor, which is the credit spread. The model design and the corresponding assumptions are the core challenge of this thesis.

Arvanitis et al. (1999) argue that a jump-diffusion model is able to simulate the properties of credit spreads. Consequently, a Cox-Ingersoll-Ross (CIR) process is used for the diffusion part and a compound Poison process for the jump component.

Stefano Iacus and Nakahiro Yoshida provide the technical means for the Monte Carlo simulation with their freely available R package YUIMA. As a complementing documentation they published a detailed framework for working with YUIMA.

Jorion (2011), Iacus/Yoshida (2018) and Hull (2018) are cited sources for the description of the CIR process and its comparison to other interest rate models.

Castagna/Fede (2013), Ross (1996) and Alt (2010) provide the details on the compound Poisson process.

In Chapter 6 the case calculation for a hypothetical Austrian bank is performed. The input data is listed and the use of YUIMA package explained.

The simplified liquidity balance sheet is an artificial example created for the use within this thesis. It does not base on real data, but the inflows and outflows are constructed in a way that they show a common gap structure of universal banks.

The data on EUR swap rates and Austrian sovereign credit default swap (CDS) spreads is real information and was provided by the author's employer. The sovereign CDS spreads are used as a proxy for the institution specific CDS spreads of an Austrian bank.

In Section 6.3 the parameters for the CIR component are estimated with YUIMA package in a way that they fit to the observed history of credit spreads. An independent estimation of parameters for each of the required tenors (6M, 1Y, 2Y, 3Y, 4Y and 5Y) is performed.

Subsection 6.3.1 is dedicated to the estimation of the jump intensity to be used for the simulation. The proposed approach is to derive the jump intensity from a rating transition matrix. The jump intensity should represent the expected number of rating downgrades within 1 year or 250 trading days.

After all required parameters are defined, the Monte Carlo simulation of credit spreads is explained in Section 6.4. The 99.9% quantile of the simulation result represents the stressed credit spread.

In Subsection 6.5 the simulation result is then used as part of the funding costs to discount the open liquidity positions from the given liquidity balance sheet. The present values of the liquidity gaps are calculated first under the assumption of normal funding costs and then using the stressed funding costs. A comparison of the figures will show the effect of the simulated scenario and if there is need to hold economic capital. As mentioned previously, the concept of discounting open liquidity positions is adopted from Enthofer/Haas (2018).

In Subsection 6.5.1 and 6.5.2 a differing gap structure from alternative liquidity balance sheets is used to check the effect on the result of the quantification of structural liquidity risk.

A summary of results and findings, as well as a critical discussion of the model and its assumptions is presented in Chapter 7.

Liquidity and Risk

2

Liquidity is a qualitative element of the financial strength of an institution. It represents the capacity to fulfill obligations when they fall due. If the bank lacks this ability, it will find itself in the condition of illiquidity.[1]

The relationship between solvency and liquidity is close. An institution's solvency is a precondition for its liquidity. Solvency describes a condition of capital adequacy, in which there is a sufficient amount of capital to cover losses, while liquidity is only cash related.[2]

2.1 Categories of Liquidity

The views on liquidity in Figure 2.1 are addressed by liquidity risk management with a special focus on the first two types.

2.2 Liquidity Risk

Liquidity risk arises from a bank's (in-)ability to meet its financial obligations when they come due, without incurring unacceptable losses, that may result from high funding costs.[3]

This risk arises as the bank might not be able to meet both expected and unexpected current and future cashflows and collateral needs efficiently. Liquidity needs can occur, for instance, if planned refinancing can only be obtained at

[1] Duttweiler (2009) pp. 1–2

[2] Duttweiler (2009) pp. 10–11

[3] Basel Committee on Banking Supervision (2008) p. 1

C. Wieser, *Quantification of Structural Liquidity Risk in Banks*, BestMasters,
https://doi.org/10.1007/978-3-658-39593-3_2

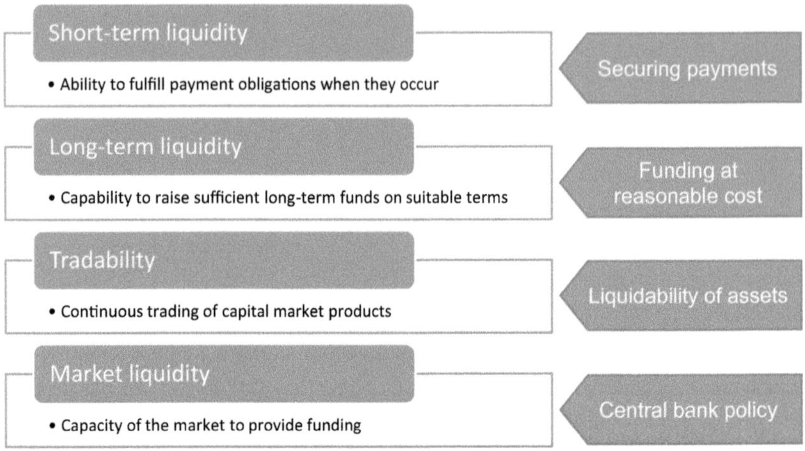

Figure 2.1 Different types of liquidity[4]

very adverse terms or is entirely impossible, if repayments in credit business are not made on time, or if committed lines are unexpectedly drawn or deposits unexpectedly withdrawn on a large scale. In case of a liquidity shortfall, the bank might incur losses out of different reasons:

- the bank's funding costs might increase disproportionately,
- a lack of funding can prevent the bank from making new business,
- or the bank might be unable to settle payments in due time.

According to this definition and examples of liquidity risk the timeframe is an important characteristic.[5]

Additionally, there are other dimensions to categorize liquidity risk in Figure 2.2.

[4] Bartetzky et al. (2008) p. 9

[5] Ruozi/Ferrari (2013) p. 11

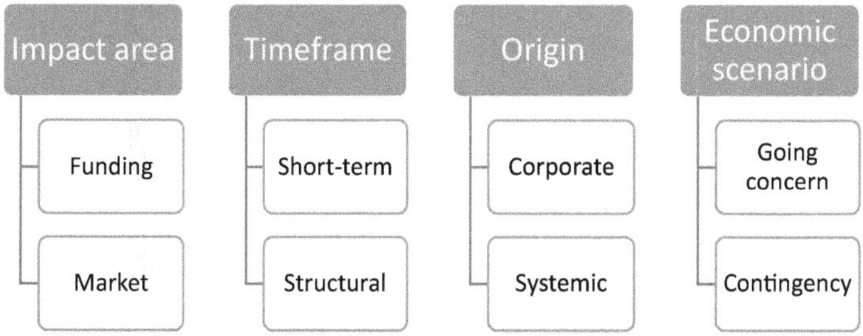

Figure 2.2 Dimensions of liquidity risk[6]

2.2.1 Short-term Liquidity Risk

Short-term liquidity risk is defined as risk of the bank not being able to meet its financial obligations when they become due. It typically arises from term and currency transformation, when the bank funds long term assets with short term liabilities, or it significantly misjudges the liquidity of its balance sheet positions:[7]

- Errors in modelling haircuts on securities
- Misjudgment of stickiness on customer deposits
- Unexpectedly high drawing on commitments

Then the cumulated cash outflows might exceed cumulated cash inflows over a certain time horizon. A similar problem can arise when currencies are not freely convertible and the cash inflow in a particular currency has to be converted into a cash outflow in another currency.

2.2.2 Long-term Liquidity Risk

Long-term or structural liquidity risk is defined as the risk of a loss as necessary funding transactions might be only achievable on less favorable terms.

Structural liquidity risk arises as funding costs and supply move with the bank's credit spread that is subject to change. It may also arise from a significant

[6] Ruozi/Ferrari (2013) p. 10

[7] Bartetzky et al. (2008) pp. 9–13

change in the composition of liabilities, mainly from higher dependence on interbank funding when customer deposits are withdrawn and cannot be rolled over or renewed.[8]

2.3 Interdependency of Liquidity Risk

The majority of risks in banking have an influence on liquidity, hence it is not a driving but more a subsequent element (Figure 2.3).[9]

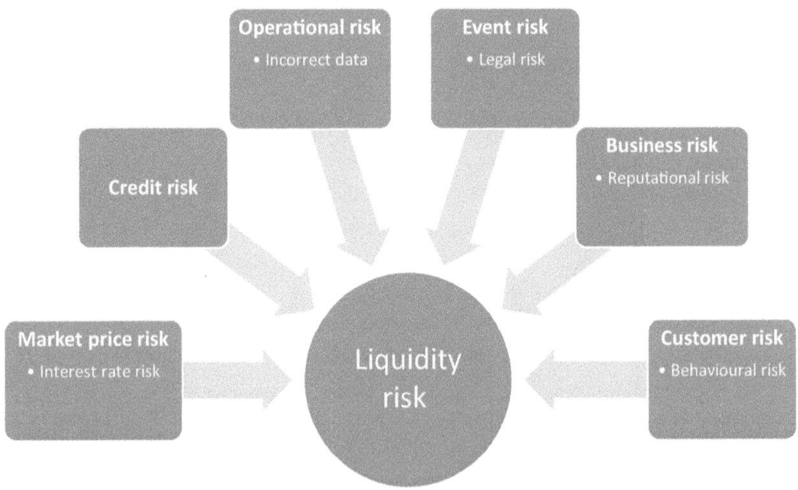

Figure 2.3 Interdependency of liquidity risk[10]

The interactions with other types of risks led to an alternative classification of liquidity risk into derivative and original.[11]

[8] Bartetzky et al. (2008) pp. 9–13
[9] Duttweiler (2009) p. 3
[10] Bartetzky et al. (2008) p. 11
[11] Schierenbeck (2008) pp. 514–515

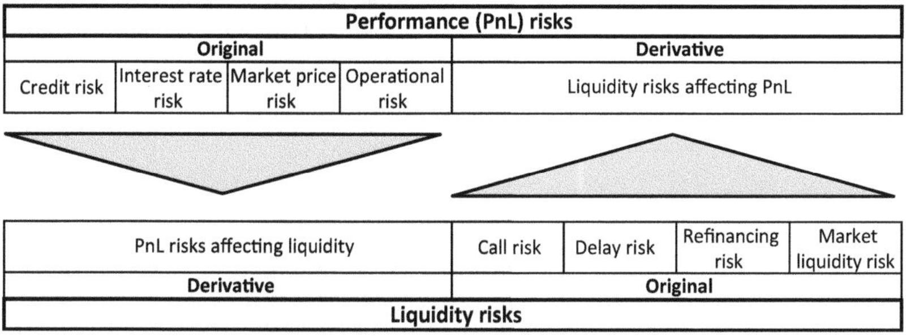

Figure 2.4 Derivative and original liquidity risks and their relationship to PnL risks

The call risk (translated from German term "Abrufrisiko") in Figure 2.4 is described as the risk of unexpected drawing of credit lines or unexpected deposit outflow. The risk of expected contractual payments (cash inflows) being deferred is defined as delay risk (translated from German term "Terminrisiko").

2.4 Liquidity versus Interest Rate Risk

Gap analysis is important for the measurement of both liquidity and interest rate risk. As long as the maturity of a product is the same as the term with fixed interest, gap analysis will produce the same results. This is only the case for some simple products without optionalities (like early repayment, bonds with call feature, etc.), but not for the majority of products. Adjustments of interest rates during the lifetime of a product cause the gaps to differ.[12]

The second important characteristic of liquidity risk is that there are no derivatives. Hedging of interest rate risk is not a problem with products like futures, swaps and options. While liquidity risk focuses on cashflows only, interest rate risk management does not exclusively use cash instruments. When utilizing derivatives to steer interest rate risk, no principal payments are involved. Interest rate risk can be created solely through derivatives and without any principal position showing up on the liquidity balance sheet.[13]

[12] Bartetzky (2008) p. 31

[13] Duttweiler (2009) pp. 11–14

Liquidity Risk Regulation 3

A key aspect of the Basel III reform after the financial crisis of 2007/08 is liquidity risk management. Within Basel III the first internationally harmonized set of liquidity standards was introduced with the following ratios and metrics:

- Liquidity Coverage Ratio (LCR)
- Net Stable Funding Ratio (NSFR)
- Additional Monitoring Metrics (ALMM)

The first standards on LCR and NSFR were published in 2010 with the title "Basel III: International framework for liquidity risk measurement, standards and monitoring" by the Basel Committee on Banking Supervision (BCBS). After an observation period that allowed for revisions the final rules were set in January 2013 for LCR and October 2014 for NSFR.[1]

3.1 Liquidity Coverage Ratio

This section is based on the publication "Basel III: The Liquidity Coverage Ratio and liquidity risk monitoring tools" of the BCBS dated January 2013.[2]

The LCR assumes a short-term stress scenario lasting for 30 days where estimated net cash outflows must be covered by high quality liquid assets to ensure the survival of the institution.

The requirement is shown by the following inequality:

---

[1] Venkat/Baird (2013) p. 213

[2] Basel Committee on Banking Supervision (2013) n.pag.

C. Wieser, *Quantification of Structural Liquidity Risk in Banks*, BestMasters,
https://doi.org/10.1007/978-3-658-39593-3_3

$$\frac{High-quality\ liquid\ assets(HQLA)}{Total\ net\ cash\ outflows\ over\ the\ next\ 30\ days} \geq 100\% \tag{3.1}$$

The 30-day liquidity stress scenario is defined with following characteristics:

- Three-notch downgrade of the institution's credit rating
- Partial withdrawal of retail deposits
- Limited availability of unsecured wholesale refinancing
- Partial loss of secured short-term funding with increased haircuts for secured funding
- Substantial liquidity needs for collateral calls and drawings of committed credit lines and other off-balance sheet exposures

The Basel III framework provides a catalogue of assumptions for haircuts on HQLAs and cashflows of maturing balance sheet items. Only the treatment of guarantees and letters of credit are subject to national supervision, whereas the most factors are given in the BCBS framework.

3.1.1 Liquid Assets

High-quality liquid assets (HQLA) are assets that provide mitigating effects in stress periods because they can be liquidated at any time with little to no loss of value.

HQLA must meet the following criteria:[3]

3.1.1.1 Fundamental Characteristics

- Low risk: high credit quality and seniority increase an asset's liquidity, as well as low duration (referring to interest rate risk) and low foreign exchange risk
- Ease and certainty of valuation: standardized and simply structured assets are more fungible, which promotes liquidity. Pricing formulas for HQLAs must not depend on strong assumptions.
- Low correlation with risky assets
- Listed on a developed and recognized exchange

[3] Basel Committee on Banking Supervision (2013) p. 13

3.1.1.2 Market-related Characteristics

- Active and sizable market: evidenced by low bid-ask spreads, high trading volumes and many market participants
- Low volatility: history of stable prices, haircuts and volumes also during stressed periods
- Flight to quality: observed tendencies to move into these assets in previous crises

3.1.1.3 Liquid Assets classified into three Levels according to their Quality

- Level 1 is limited to cash, central bank reserves and high-quality sovereign bonds
- Level 2 consists of two sublevels and must not be more than 40% of the overall stock after haircuts applied

    - A: securities guaranteed by sovereigns, corporate and covered bonds that meet certain conditions
    - B: residential mortgage backed securities, corporate debt and common equity shares that satisfy certain conditions, as well as certain additional assets subject to the discretion of the national authorities

Level 1 assets are not subject to haircuts, but on Level 2 A (15%) and 2B (25–50%) haircuts are applicable.

3.1.2 Outflows

The stress scenario mentioned above simulated by applying different outflow rates on different types of liabilities and off-balance positions:

- Retail deposits
    - Stable
    - Less/Non-Stable

- Unsecured wholesale funding provided by
  - small business customers
  - operational deposits for clearing, custody and cash management activities
  - a network of cooperative banks
  - non-financial corporates and sovereigns
  - other legal entities
- Secured funding (differentiation in backing asset levels)
- Undrawn committed facilities (differentiation in client segments)
- Derivatives

3.1.3 Inflows

Contractual inflows including interest from performing outstanding exposure may be considered, but there is a cap on total inflows. Inflows are only allowed to offset 75% of total expected cash outflows. This should ensure that there is a minimum stock of HQLA held by the institution.

Similar to the outflow rates above, inflow rates are applied on the other types of inflows e.g. from secured lending transactions depending on their backing asset level.

3.2 Net Stable Funding Ratio

This section is based on the publication "Basel III: the net stable funding ratio" of the BCBS dated October 2014.[4]

The net stable funding ratio (NSFR) was proposed by the BCBS to ensure sufficient long-term and stable funding for less liquid and longer-term assets.

The NSFR is calculated the following:

$$\frac{Available\ stable\ funding(ASF)}{Required\ stable\ funding(RSF)} \geq 100\% \tag{3.2}$$

[4] Basel Committee on Banking Supervision (2014)

3.2.1 Available Stable Funding

ASF measures the liabilities expected to be reliable for over one year. Own capital and long-term wholesale funding (without optionality to be withdrawn prior to maturity) contribute to ASF. On the other hand, there is the experience of the financial crisis which has shown that short-term wholesale funding is less reliable. The required rollover of short-term funding was highly problematic during the financial crisis of 2007/08.[5]

There are five different categories of ASF that are multiplied with different factors according to their reliability, which is mentioned in Table 3.1.

Table 3.1 Selected liabilities and corresponding available stable funding (ASF) factors[6]

ASF factor	Components of ASF category
100%	Total regulatory capital (excluding Tier 2 instruments with residual maturity of less than one year) Other liabilities with effective residual maturity of one year or more
95%	Stable demand deposits and term deposits with residual maturity of less than one year provided by retail and small business customers
90%	Less stable demand deposits and term deposits with residual maturity of less than one year provided by retail and small business customers
50%	Funding with residual maturity of less than one year provided by non-financial corporate customers Operational deposits Funding with residual maturity of less than one year from sovereigns, public sector entities and development banks Other funding with residual maturity between six months and less than one year not included in the above categories, including funding provided by central banks and financial institutions
0%	All other liabilities and equity not included in the above categories, including liabilities without a stated maturity (with a specific treatment for deferred tax liabilities and minority interests) NSFR derivative liabilities net of NSFR derivative assets (if NSFR derivative liabilities are greater than NSFR derivative assets)

[5] Venkat/Baird (2013) p. 226

[6] Basel Committee on Banking Supervision (2014) p. 6

3.2.2 Required Stable Funding

RSF measures the liquidity and maturity of the assets. The liquidity characteristic is not only about the ability to sell the asset, but also about the ability to repo those assets. The probability to be able to sell a portfolio of long-term retail loans is smaller compared to securities traded on liquid markets. Some less liquid instruments may only be sold with a significant haircut and thus require a higher amount of stable funding, as stated in Table 3.2.

Table 3.2 Selected assets and off-balance items with corresponding ASF factors

RSF factor	Components of RSF category
0%	Cash, central bank reserves and claims with less than 6 months residual maturity
5%	Unencumbered assets of Level 1 (excl. above components)[7]
10%	Unencumbered loans to financial institutions with less than 6 months residual maturity and specific collateral
15%	Other unencumbered loans to financial institutions with less than 6 months residual maturity Unencumbered assets of Level 2 A
50%	Unencumbered assets of Level 2B Loans to FI and CB with less than 12 months residual maturity Operational deposits at other FI Other assets with less than 12 months residual maturity
65%	Mortgage and other unencumbered loans (non-FI) with low risk weight ($\leq$ 35% under standardized approach) and residual maturity of more than 12 months
85%	Other unencumbered performing loans (non-FI), exchange-traded securities and commodities
100%	Other assets and derivatives (under special rules)
	Off-balance items with factors determined by national supervisors, except for an RSF factor of 5% for irrevocable and conditionally revocable credit facilities

Before the crisis of 2007/08 many institutions funded their long-term loan books to a great extent through short-term wholesale funding like interbank deposits. This type of funding is not stable and reliable in times of crises. To

[7] Asset level classification introduced in Section 3.1.1

tackle the problems arising from such balance sheet structures the BCBS introduced the NSFR. The NSFR is also a necessary complement to the LCR that only focuses on the short term and may provide adverse incentives for the medium and long term.[8]

3.3 Additional (Liquidity) Monitoring Metrics

To obtain a comprehensive view of an institution's liquidity risk profile and liquidity risk trends the national competent authorities demand additional metrics. Article 415(3)(b) of the CRR required the EBA to develop draft Implementing Technical Standards (ITS), which were first published in April 2014.[9]

Following metrics were proposed and later also implemented:

- **Contractual maturity ladder with time buckets for up to 10 years:**
  Maturity mismatch of the contractual flows should be shown as gaps for defined time buckets without application of behavioral models
- **Concentration of funding by counterparty:**
  This template lists the counterparties, products and additional information when the funding from this source exceeds the threshold of 1% of total liabilities
- **Concentration of funding by product type:**
  This template lists the product types that provide a funding amount of more than 1% of total liabilities split into retail and wholesale funding
- **Prices for various lengths of funding:**
  Several time buckets ranging from overnight to 10 years show average volumes and prices of funding transactions
- **Rollover of funding:**
  This template shows which volume of funds matured and how much new funding was raised in the reported month
- **Concentration of counterbalancing capacity by issuer/counterparty:**
  This section collects data on the 10 largest sources of counterbalancing capacity[10]

[8] Venkat/Baird (2013) pp. 226–227

[9] European Banking Authority (2014) p. 3

[10] European Banking Authority (2014) pp. 3–4

3.4 SREP: ICAAP and ILAAP

Within the supervisory review and evaluation process (SREP) described in Pillar 2 of the Basel framework the institution's internal processes ICAAP and ILAAP are assessed. The supervisor examines the plans, processes and systems that ensure a sufficient amount of economic capital and liquidity.[11]

The internal capital adequacy and assessment process (ICAAP) is implemented to determine material risks of loss. Those risks must be identified, measured, reported and controlled as mentioned in Chapter 1 (Figure 3.1).

Figure 3.1 Stages of ICAAP process[12]

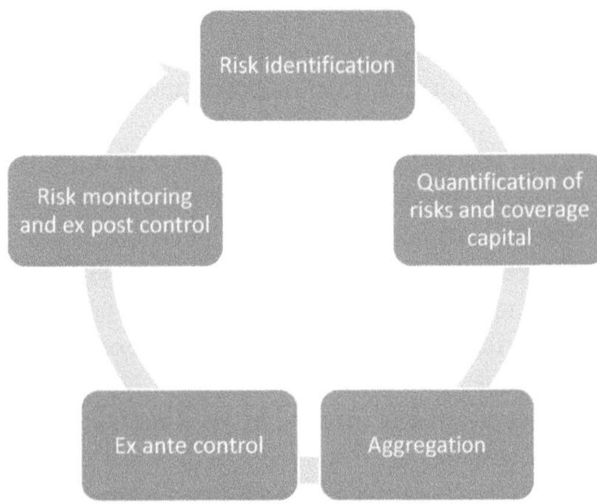

The ICAAP differentiates three scenarios:[13]

- Going concern: ensure a minimum annual result to preserve the capital level
  - measurement of PnL risks
- Gone concern—liquidation: ensure coverage of debt
  - measurement of all significant risks
- Gone concern—stress scenario: ensure financial coverage of equity
  - Similar risk scope as in liquidation approach, different scenarios

[11] Enthofer/Haas (2018) p. 124

[12] Thonabauer/Nösslinger (2006) p. 68

[13] Enthofer/Haas (2018) pp. 116–122

The differences in scope of going concern versus liquidation approach are depicted in Figure 3.2: Going concern is about the preservation of equity capital while in the liquidation approach it is used as a buffer.

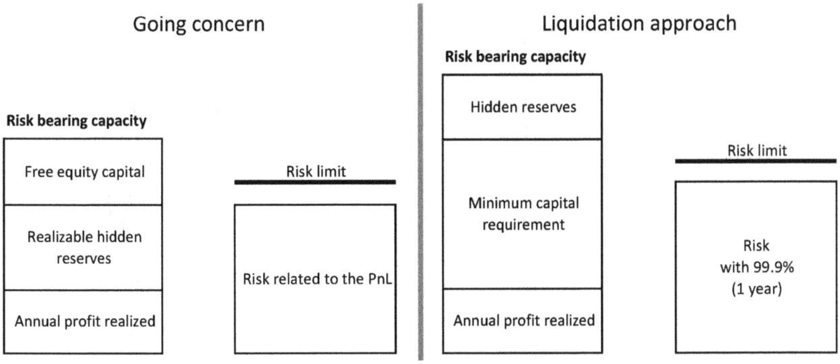

Figure 3.2 Going concern vs. liquidation approach[14]

Article 107 of CRD IV describes all the risk to be included in the ICAAP. Some risks may be irrelevant to specific institutions and for exclusion a comprehensive argumentation is required. Also, additional institution specific risks must be identified.

Within SREP the supervisory authority also assesses the institution's procedures for determination of adequate liquidity buffers. This procedure is the internal liquidity adequacy and assessment process (ILAAP).[15]

3.4.1 The Concept of Economic Capital

Economic capital is the amount of capital required to absorb unexpected losses over a prescribed time horizon. Expected losses represented by the statistical mean are covered by reserves and provisions. Expected losses are also included in the pricing policy.[16]

[14] Enthofer/Haas (2018) p. 118

[15] Enthofer/Haas (2018) p. 222

[16] Porteous/Tapadar (2006) p. 45

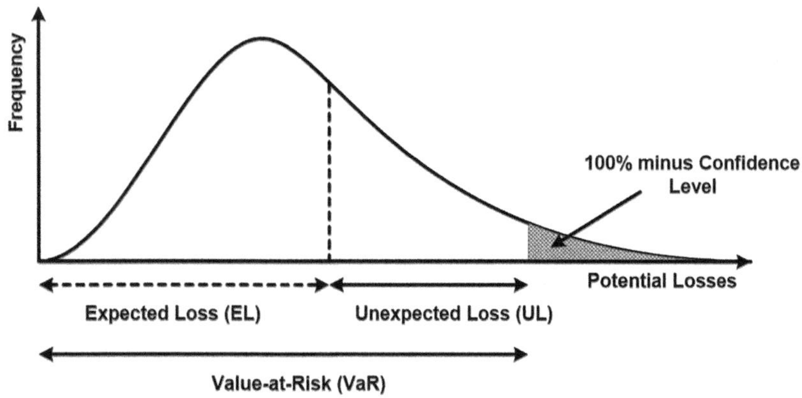

Figure 3.3 Expected versus unexpected loss[17]

Unexpected loss is the total loss in excess of the mean loss when a downside tail event occurs, as shown in Figure 3.3. Tail events rarely occur, but when they do their impact is severe. The function of economic (and regulatory) capital is to provide a buffer against the tail event's impact to protect the institution's creditors.[18]

3.4.1.1 Regulatory and Economic Capital differ in their Framework

Regulatory capital regulation is described in Pillar 1 of the Basel Accords on banking supervision. Within Pillar 1, the minimum regulatory capital requirements are calculated for credit, market and operational risk.[19]

The economic capital calculations are described in Pillar 2 and the focus is on all material risks the institution is exposed to, as already stated in Section 3.4.

---

[17] Basel Committee on Banking Supervision (2005) p. 3

[18] Basel Committee on Banking Supervision (2005) p. 2

[19] Barfield et al. (2011) p. 10

Liquidity Risk Management 4

This chapter describes the tools and models used to measure and manage liquidity risk in banks.

4.1 Liquidity Balance Sheet

A fundamental tool in managing liquidity risk is the liquidity balance sheet, which is all about expected future cashflows from a specific point of view, the reference date.[1]

4.1.1 Stock and Flow Perspective

The link between balance sheet items and cashflows can be described from different perspectives. The stock perspective is represented by the balance sheet and the flow perspective by cashflows, which are changes in the stock of balance sheet items. Liabilities are generating outflows and assets are generating incoming cashflows.[2]

Future cashflows can be classified using the two dimensions time and amount, both with a deterministic and a stochastic category, as shown in Figure 4.1.[3]

[1] Bartetzky et al. (2008) p. 13

[2] Schmaltz (2009) p. 25

[3] Castagna/Fede (2013) p. 112

C. Wieser, *Quantification of Structural Liquidity Risk in Banks*, BestMasters,
https://doi.org/10.1007/978-3-658-39593-3_4

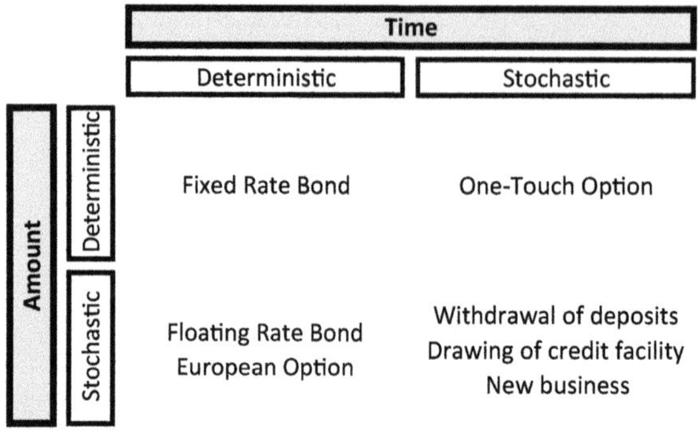

Figure 4.1 Taxonomy of cashflows

4.1.2 Maturity Ladder

In a next step the balance sheet items are categorized according to their maturity, as well as the cashflows (into a maturity ladder). Volume and maturity mismatches are already shown in the maturity structured balance sheet but are better visible in the maturity ladder of cashflows (Figure 4.2).[4]

The cashflow maturity ladder can be represented as liquidity balance sheet, which is the standard term for the concept of maturity ladder within this thesis (example in Table 6.1).

As described in Figure 4.1 the cashflows may be stochastic and therefore need to be modelled for creating a maturity ladder of cashflows. Such models are referred to as behavioral models because they consider also other factors than only standard rationality principles.

The three major fields of application for behavioral models are: prepayments, sight deposits (and other non-maturing liabilities) and credit line drawings.[5]

4.1.3 Modelling of Sight Deposits

In the financial literature two approaches for modelling the evolution of deposit balances can be found:[6]

[4] Schmaltz (2009) p. 26

[5] Castagna/Fede (2013) p. 277

[6] Castagna/Fede (2013) pp. 317–319

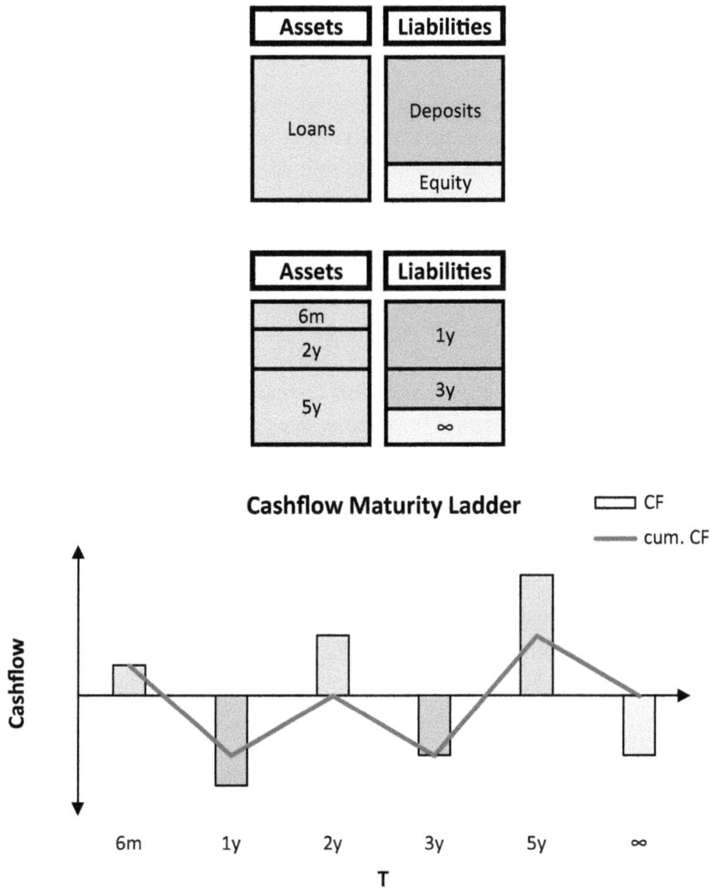

Figure 4.2 Translating the balance sheet into a maturity ladder

4.1.3.1 Bond Portfolio Replication

Bond portfolio replication splits the total deposits into two parts:

- The core part is assumed to be insensitive towards interest rates and other market variables' evolution. This part of total deposits is supposed to decrease gradually over medium to long-term period.

- The volatile part is assumed to decrease by withdrawal over a short period. This part is used by clients to satisfy their usual liquidity needs.

The replication portfolio invests the parts in bonds and money market products that match their amortization schedule, which are very short-term assets for the volatile part. The core problem of this approach is the estimation of the amortization schedule, which is done by statistical methods without incorporating stochastic risk factors.

4.1.3.2 OAS Approach

The option-adjusted spread (OAS) approach on the other hand identifies statistically how the deposit volumes react to risk factors, that are modelled as stochastic variables. OAS models have three common components: a stochastic process for interest rates, a stochastic model for deposit rates and a model for the evolution of deposit volumes.

4.1.4 Modelling of Prepayments

Early repayment of loans must be considered in liquidity risk management as it influences the cashflow maturity ladder. There are two basic approaches in modelling prepayments:[7]

4.1.4.1 Empirical Models

Past prepayment rates or other variables are used as explanatory variables for the current prepayment. Their performance is unclear for different economic environments, as the function of this set of explanatory variables is only a reduced-form representation for some real underlying process.

4.1.4.2 Rational Prepayment Models

Prepayments are modelled as options, which will be exercised when the market value of the loan is higher than the nominal residual value, which is driven by the evolution of interest rates. As not all debtors have the skills or take the time to evaluate on a regular basis, whether exercising the option makes economic sense, rational prepayment models do not closely match observed behavior.

There is empirical evidence for following features:

[7] Castagna/Fede (2013) pp. 277–278

- Prepayment even occurs for mortgages with lower coupon rates than current market rates
- Prepayment options are not exercised for all mortgages with higher coupon rates than current market rates
- Dependence on a burnout factor, which describes that prepayment rates slow down in a continuing downward trend in interest rates.
- Burnout is also a term to describe adverse selection in a mortgage portfolio: strong debtors exercise the option, whereas weaker debtors do not as they expect more expensive refinancing.[8]

Basic rational prepayment models are unable to reflect the listed features, consequently the majority of financial institutions apply empirical models. The outcome of such a model is referred to as constant prepayment rate (CPR), which can be expressed as a function of variables.

A simple form of the Richard and Roll model is represented in Equation 4.1 below:

$$CPR = f(RefinanceIncentive) * g(Seasoning) * h(Month) * l(BurnoutFactor) \tag{4.1}$$

According to Richard and Roll the CPR depends on four functions of factors, where the most important one is the refinance incentive. The resulting CPR from this empirical model provides the basis for predicting cashflows, hedging and (mortgage) pricing.[9]

4.1.5 Modelling of Loan Commitments

Credit lines or liquidity facilities are a very popular form of lending in banking business. The requirements towards models are high:

- Option for multiple withdrawals and only partial use of credit lines
- Dependencies between default probability and withdrawals
- Stochastic interest rates and default intensities
- Other influences not linked to creditworthiness

---

[8] Schultz (2016) pp. 140–141

[9] Castagna/Fede (2013) pp. 277–316

From an option point of view, the debtor is long on its own credit spread, where the strike price is at the contract spread level set at inception. This encourages approaches incorporating a stochastic model for the probability of default.[10]

4.1.6 New Business and the Concept of Stickiness

For the construction of a going concern or business as usual liquidity balance sheet, future new business should be considered as well. New business may be contracted on both sides of the bank's balance sheet and the cashflows are stochastic in time and amount, which makes it especially difficult to model and manage.[11]

The concept of stickiness deals for example with the situation of maturing term deposits. Especially for retail term deposits, the likelihood is high that they are not fully withdrawn at maturity, but that a high fraction remains as sight deposit or is rolled over/renewed as term deposit.[12]

4.1.7 Counterbalancing Capacity (CBC)

Counterbalancing capacity refers to all possible strategies to generate incoming cashflows. Contractual cashflows are not considered, as CBC is about the generation of inflows above a business-as-usual scenario. CBC has a broader definition compared to the concept of liquidity buffer.[13]

---

[10] Castagna/Fede (2013) pp. 337–338

[11] Castagna/Fede (2013) p. 113

[12] Duttweiler (2009) p. 253

[13] Castagna/Fede (2013) pp. 143–144

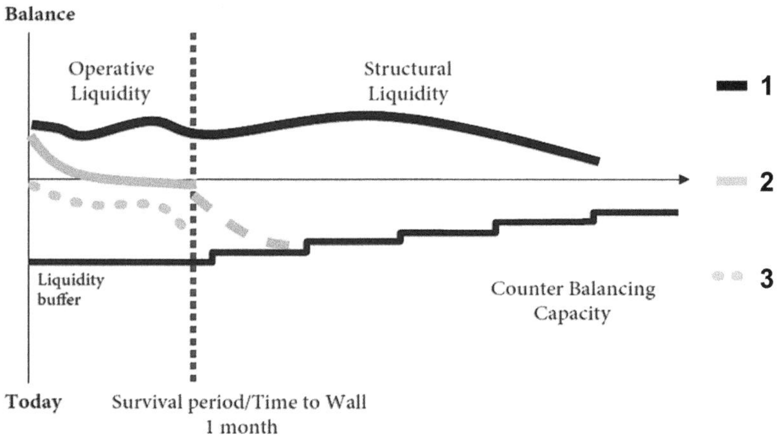

Figure 4.3 Effect of liquidity buffers[14]

Three different scenarios for the cumulated gaps are depicted in Figure 4.3:

The first curve shows a business as usual case with expected new business included, whereas the second one does not include new business.

The third curve represents a stress event, which can be simulated by one of the approaches introduced in the next Section 1.2 about stress testing. Within stress scenarios the importance of the liquidity buffer is highlighted. There must be a sufficient amount of central bank eligible assets at disposal to ensure a minimum survival period in stress.[15]

4.2 Stress Testing

Scenarios are very important in liquidity risk. Measurement of liquidity risk has a higher dependency on scenario analysis than credit or operational risk.[16]

One standardized scenario in liquidity risk measurement is introduced in Section 3.1, namely the LCR.

Liquidity stress testing is based on the projection of cashflows arising from assets, liabilities and off-balance sheet positions under systemic, idiosyncratic and

[14] Enthofer/Haas (2018) p. 898.

[15] Enthofer/Haas (2018) pp. 896–900

[16] Matz et al. (2007) p. 37

combined scenarios over varying time horizons. Stress testing results provide the basis for determining the institution's liquidity risk appetite, setting limits and developing a contingency funding plan.[17]

4.2.1 Approaches in Stress Testing

Stress testing techniques can be separated in three approaches:

- **Deterministic models:**
  Stress scenario with fixed assumptions (e.g. on outflow rates)
  Parameters set by expert opinion and analysis of past stress events
- **Historical statistical:**
  Cashflow modelling based on observed volatility
- **Monte Carlo simulation:**
  Statistical simulation techniques for stressing variables over a specified timespan

As liquidity stress is a typical high impact/low probability ("tail") event deterministic scenarios are considered most effective, despite their reliance on numerous assumptions.[18]

4.2.2 Scenario Characteristics

Financial institutions typically develop several liquidity stress scenarios that are either idiosyncratic (only institution specific) or systemic. A drop in market liquidity would be systemic, whereas a reputational crisis is an idiosyncratic scenario. A combined or concurrent scenario adopts features of both categories. Liquidity scenarios further differ in their level of severity, impact assumption on counterparties or products, and whether they are a regulatory requirement.

Instead of calculating a stress scenario based on assumptions, reverse stress testing may be performed. The goal of a reverse stress test is to find and list conditions that would cause the bank's current business plan to fail. Factors with

[17] Venkat/Baird (2013) p. 27

[18] Venkat/Baird (2013) p. 37

the most significant impact on the bank's liquidity need to be determined and stressed to a destructive extent.[19]

4.2.3 Stress Testing Conclusions

Liquidity stress testing is supposed to deliver several outputs in a regular reporting package. The survival period or time to wall is the most prominent outcome of liquidity stress testing.[20] Should the survival period drop under the limit, which causes a limit breach a certain chain of actions is triggered:

- 1st level: reporting of breach to Treasury and the Board
  Liquidity manager must explain the cause and initiate countermeasures within a time limit
- 2nd level: if the breach was not fixed in time in 1st level
  Treasury investigates causes and proposes remedies
- 3rd level: if the breach has still not been fixed
  Escalation to asset-liability committee (ALCO) to decide on measures and restructuring[21]

4.3 Intraday Liquidity Risk Management

Intraday liquidity is defined as the funds that can be accessed during the business day. Those funds are usually used to make payments in real time. There is the risk that the bank fails to manage its intraday liquidity leaving it unable to make a payment in time. This situation affects the bank's as well as the counterparty's liquidity position.[22]

4.3.1 Sources and Usage of Intraday Liquidity

Own sources of intraday liquidity are reserve balances at the central bank, collateral pledged with the central bank or other payment systems and credit lines

[19] Venkat/Baird (2013) pp. 39–40

[20] Venkat Baird (2013) pp. 44–46

[21] Matz et al. (2007) p. 84

[22] Basel Committee on Banking Supervision (2013) p. 3

with intraday availability. Other sources are received payments from participants in the payment system.

The typical usage of mentioned sources is for payments to participants in the payment systems and for drawings of offered intraday credit lines.[23]

4.3.2 Monitoring Tools

There are different sets of monitoring tools applicable to banks according to their role in the payment system. The following indicators apply to all reporting banks:[24]

- Daily maximum intraday liquidity usage, which is the largest negative cumulative position
- Available intraday liquidity at start
- Total payments made and received
- Time-specific obligations, which have intraday settlement deadlines

4.4 Early Warning Indicators

By the principles for sound liquidity risk management published by the BCBS financial institutions are required to design a set of indicators for the identification of trends towards increasing liquidity needs or vulnerabilities.

Early warning indicators (EWIs) can be qualitative as well as quantitative indicators:

- Concentration of funding
- Concentration of lending business
- Weighted average maturity of liabilities
- Number of limit breaches in stress testing
- Rating downgrade
- Price movements of the institution's shares
- CDS spread widening

[23] Basel Committee on Banking Supervision (2013) pp. 3–4

[24] Castagna/Fede (2013) p. 71

- LCR or NSFR development[25]

Risk monitoring with the help of EWIs was significantly increased after the 2007/08 financial crisis. Financial institutions must ensure that EWIs are refined and updated as part of the liquidity risk management framework.[26]

4.5 Contingency Planning

The stress tests and early warning indicators must be linked as (automatic) triggers to the contingency funding plan (CFP).[27]

The CFP is a set of well-organized action plans for minimizing and managing potential crises and comprises following aspects:

- Separate action plans for different crisis environments
- Well-established early warning system
- Specific guidance on tackling hypothetical crisis events defined in advance
- The CFP should not overweight crisis events in the recent past
- The plan should leave flexibility and not be too detailed
- Separate plan for each material currency
- Well-defined responsibilities of the governing bodies
- Communication plans and higher frequency reporting[28]

The contingency funding plan is a playbook that needs regular updating, as its effectiveness lies in the operational readiness.[29]

[25] Basel Committee on Banking Supervision (2008) p. 16

[26] Venkat/Baird (2013) p. 129

[27] Enthofer/Haas (2018) p. 844

[28] Matz et al. (2007) pp. 126–129

[29] Venkat/Baird (2016) p. 124

4.6 Stochastic Model Concepts

Besides the gap analyses derived from maturity ladders, there are also stochastic model concepts in liquidity risk measurement (Figure 4.4).[30]

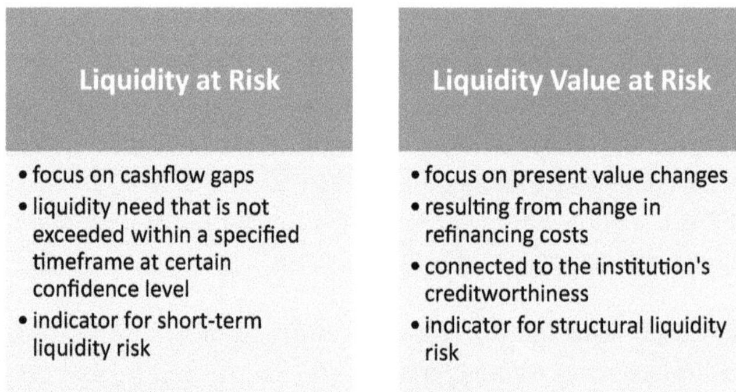

Figure 4.4 Stochastic model concepts: LaR vs LVaR[31]

4.6.1 Liquidity at Risk

Liquidity at risk (LaR) measures the shortfall in net cashflows that will not be exceeded within a specified period at a certain confidence level. LaR may be compared to value at risk concepts in market risk, but it relates to the distribution of cash outflows and not to a PnL distribution.[32]

LaR's methodology is based on historical observations of daily cashflows and their net balance to statistically determine their distribution function. As the focus is on extraordinary events with peak outflows that rarely occur, models from extreme value theory are suggested. The resulting LaR figure needs to be covered with a sufficient amount of liquid assets.[33]

Models like the LaR which base on historical observations are criticized for their performance in the 2007/08 crisis. The reason is that historical statistical

[30] Deutsche Bundesbank (2008) p. 62

[31] Bartetzky et al. (2008) p. 28

[32] Deutsche Bundesbank (2008) p. 62

[33] Bartetzky et al. (2008) p. 126

inference is problematic for (illiquidity) risks that emerge only in environments that have been stable for a long while and suddenly drop.[34]

4.6.2 Liquidity Value at Risk

The risk of higher funding costs may be measured by using a liquidity value at risk (LVaR) approach. LVaR is supposed to determine long-term or structural liquidity risk, contrary to the LaR. While LaR needs to be covered with liquid assets, the LVaR has an impact on PnL and thus also on capital requirements.[35]

The calculation of LVaR has the following stages:[36]

1. Calculation of gaps on the liquidity balance sheet
2. Calculation of gap closing costs/profits on current terms
3. Calculation of gap closing costs/profits on changed (or stressed) terms
4. Optional inclusion of profits from realization of assets

This list of steps is similarly applied in the model proposed in Chapter 5 and 6.

In Matz et. al. (2007) the concept is referred to as value liquidity at risk and the quantification methodology is similar to the proposed model in Section 6.5.[37]

---

[34] Fiedler (2011) p. 3

[35] Deutsche Bundesbank (2008) p. 62

[36] Bartetzky et al. (2008) p. 27

[37] Matz et al. (2007) pp. 200–201

5 Model for the Quantification of Structural Liquidity Risk

This chapter introduces the concepts, tools and models, which are used to determine the amount of economic capital that is supposed to cover structural liquidity risk.

5.1 Liquidity Cost Risk[1]

There are 3 different views on the risks within ICAAP as described in Section 3.4. In each view the impact of a change in refinancing costs on PnL and eventually own funds is calculated.[2]

The proposed model focuses on the liquidation view, where the core assumption is that all open liquidity positions are closed. Based on adverse changes in the refinancing costs the economic capital or risk-bearing capacity is reduced.

Approaches within the liquidation view differ in the open positions to be closed:[3]

- all positions:
  assumes that both assets and liabilities are affected to the same extent by changed refinancing costs
- asset-gaps (positive gaps):
  closing only asset-gaps does not consider the cumulated liquidity position (neglecting time buckets with excess funding)

---

[1] Liquidity cost risk is the term used in Enthofer/Haas (2018) and comparable to LVaR described in Section 4.6.2

[2] Enthofer/Haas (2018) p. 920

[3] Enthofer/Haas (2018) p. 924

C. Wieser, *Quantification of Structural Liquidity Risk in Banks*, BestMasters,
https://doi.org/10.1007/978-3-658-39593-3_5

- cumulated asset-forward gaps:
  closing forward gaps considers the cumulated position

The approach in proposed model is to close all positions, as mitigating effects from negative gaps (excess funding) are expected. For simplicity, the impact of changed refinancing costs on both assets and liabilities is assumed to be equal.

5.2 Funding Cost Curve

The cost curve to price the closing of open liquidity positions (gaps) is constructed by adding a spread on top of the swap rates for the respective maturities (Figure 5.1).

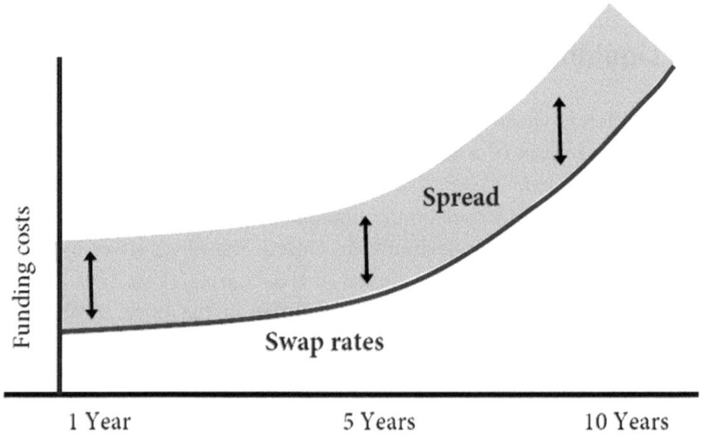

Figure 5.1 Funding cost curve[4]

The spread is derived from the CDS spreads of Austrian Government debt issues. It is assumed that a medium to large-sized Austrian bank would have to pay ten times the spread of an Austrian government debt issue.

[4] Enthofer/Haas (2018) p. 112

5.2.1 Single Risk Factor

In the proposed model the credit spread is the sole source of risk. There is no other risk factor included, as a consequence also swap rates are held constant.

The reason for an exclusion of the risk from swap rate movements, or in other words, the risk from changes of the level and shape of the interest rate term structure is, that this is subject to separate quantification in interest rate risk management.

5.3 Simulating a "Stressed" Funding Cost Curve

The simulation with a jump-diffusion model is proposed to stress the credit spread of the hypothetical Austrian bank. A jump-diffusion model is able to simulate the properties of credit spreads:[5]

- Jump component:
  Credit migrations cause jumps of the credit spread at random times
- Continuous component:
  Credit spreads are mean reverting and subject to market price changes of risk

5.4 Cox-Ingersoll-Ross Model

The model of choice for the continuous component (consisting of a drift and a diffusion part) of the credit spread is the Cox-Ingersoll-Ross (CIR) model:[6]

$$dr_t = \kappa(\theta - r_t)dt + \sigma\sqrt{r_t}dW_t \tag{5.1}$$

where:

κ is the speed of mean reversion ($0 \leq \kappa < 1$)
θ is the long-term mean ($\theta \geq 0$)
σ is the volatility measure ($\sigma \geq 0$)
W_t is a Wiener process

[5] Arvanitis et al. (1999) p. 9

[6] Jorion (2011) p. 89

5.4.1 Comparison to other Interest Rate Models

The CIR (1985) model is an extension of the Vasicek (1977) model which bases on the Ornstein-Uhlenbeck (1930) process.

The simple Ornstein-Uhlenbeck (OU) process has the following stochastic differential equation:[7]

$$dX_t = -\theta X_t dt + dW_t \tag{5.2}$$

where:

$\theta > 0$ ensures stationarity
W_t is a Wiener process
(σ is not included in the simple form of OU process)

Vasicek added the mean reverting property to the OU process:[8]

$$dX_t = (\theta_1 - \theta_2 X_t)dt + \theta_3 dW_t \tag{5.3}$$

$$dX_t = \kappa(\theta - X_t)dt + \sigma dW_t \tag{5.4}$$

Equation 5.3 is stated for the purpose of comparison, whereas Equation 5.4 is used within the course of this thesis, as its parameter explanation is straightforward (see description of Equation 5.1).

Cox, Ingersoll and Ross modified Equation 5.3 the following:

$$dX_t = (\theta_1 - \theta_2 X_t)dt + \theta_3 \sqrt{X_t} dW_t \tag{5.5}$$

with $2\theta_1 > \theta_3^2$ the process is strictly positive, or else it is nonnegative meaning it can reach the state 0.[9]

The following list of properties of the CIR model demonstrates why it is a popular choice for modelling interest rates (and credit spreads in the case of this thesis):[10]

[7] Iacus/Yoshida (2018) p. 72
[8] Iacus/Yoshida (2018) p. 73
[9] Iacus/Yoshida (2018) p. 73
[10] Hull (2018) pp. 732–733

- mean reverting
- volatility dependent on the current level (of credit spread in proposed model)
- the process does not produce negative outcomes (for the credit spread)

The Chan-Karolyi-Longstaff-Sanders (CKLS) family of models provides a good framework for comparison of previously introduced models and others with widespread use in quantitative finance (Table 5.1).

The CKLS process is specified as

$$dX_t = (\theta_1 + \theta_2 X_t)dt + \theta_3 X_t^{\theta_4} dW_t \tag{5.6}$$

where for all cases $\theta_3 > 0$.[11]

Table 5.1 Family of CKLS models[12]

	θ_1	θ_2	θ_4
Merton	Any	0	0
Ornstein-Uhlenbeck	Any	Any	0
Vasicek	Any	Any	0
Cox-Ingersoll-Ross	Any	Any	0.5
Geometric Brownian Motion	0	Any	1

5.5 Jump Component as Compound Poisson Process

The CIR model is extended to a basic affine jump-diffusion model (bAJD) the following:[13]

$$dr_t = \kappa(\theta - r_t)dt + \sigma\sqrt{r_t}dW_t + dJ_t \tag{5.7}$$

where the jump component J_t is an independent compound Poisson process with a constant jump intensity λ and an independent jump size randomly drawn from a specified distribution F:[14]

[11] Iacus/Yoshida (2018) p. 74
[12] Iacus/Yoshida (2018) p. 74
[13] Castagna/Fede (2013) p. 211
[14] Ross (1996) pp. 82–87

$$J_t = \sum_{i=1}^{N_t} X_i \tag{5.8}$$

where:

N_t is the number of events (jumps) occurring until time t distributed $N_t \sim Ps(\lambda)$
X_i is the contribution (jump size) made when event i occurs distributed $X_i \sim F$

For the proposed model distribution F of the jump size is assumed to be log-normal with zero mean and a standard deviation of 0.25, which is visualized in Figure 5.2.

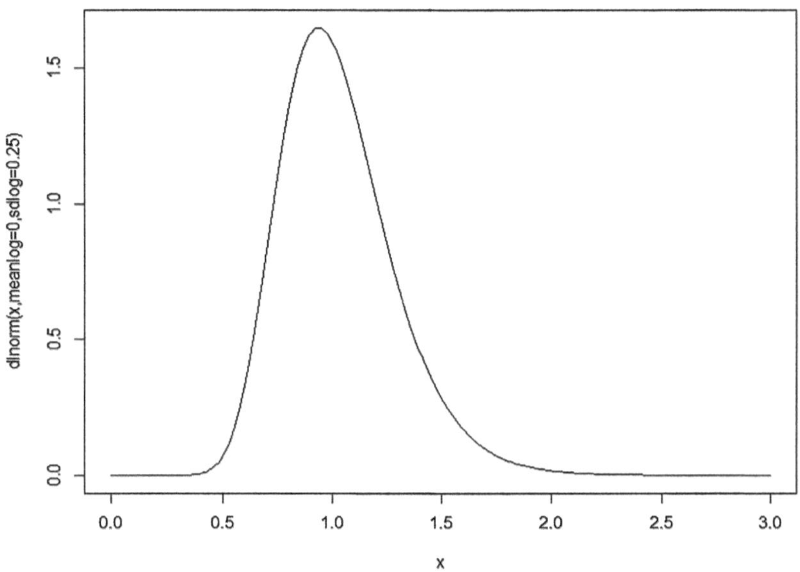

Figure 5.2 Log-normal probability density function

The reason therefore is that the compound Poisson process is intended to produce a scaling factor for the jump coefficient r_t:

$$dr_t = \kappa(\theta - r_t)dt + \sigma\sqrt{r_t}dW_t + r_t dJ_t \tag{5.9}$$

A scaling factor between 0.75 and 1.25 has a high probability to be drawn from this distribution, as visible in Figure 5.2. The according assumption for the model is that a jump event (rating downgrade) leads to a jump size between 75% and 125% of the current spread level in about 69% of jump events.

5.5.1 Properties of the Poisson Distribution

A discrete random variable X with possible values 0, 1, 2, … is Poisson distributed with parameter $\lambda > 0$ if for $k = 0, 1, 2, \ldots$ the probability mass function is of the following form:[15]

$$P(X = k) = \frac{\lambda^k}{k!} * e^{-\lambda} \tag{5.10}$$

This kind of distribution is typically applied when modelling the number of event occurrences within a specific time interval. The events occur at a constant mean rate λ and independently from each other.[16]

The properties of $X \sim Ps(\lambda)$ with the parameter $\lambda > 0$ are:

1. $E(X) = \lambda$
2. $Var(X) = \lambda$

---

[15] Alt (2010) p. 229

[16] Alt (2010) pp. 228–235

6 Calculation

This section implements the proposed model from the perspective of a medium to large-sized Austrian bank for reporting date 31.12.2019.

6.1 Input Data

Liquidity gaps from the bank's going-concern liquidity balance sheet per 31.12.2019 with underlying models for stochastic cashflows (that are approved by the regulator), as shown in Table 6.1 (and the cumulated gap structure in Figure 6.1).

Table 6.1 Liquidity balance sheet (no off-balance business)

	0–6M	6M–1Y	1–2Y	2–3Y	3–4Y	4–5Y	>5Y	Totals
Total Cash Inflows	50	25	15	15	25	25	110	265
Cash	15	0	0	0	0	0	0	15
Loans	30	20	10	10	20	20	100	210
Securities	5	5	5	5	5	5	10	40

(continued)

Supplementary Information The online version contains supplementary material available at https://doi.org/10.1007/978-3-658-39593-3_6.

C. Wieser, *Quantification of Structural Liquidity Risk in Banks*, BestMasters,
https://doi.org/10.1007/978-3-658-39593-3_6

Table 6.1 (continued)

	0–6M	6M–1Y	1–2Y	2–3Y	3–4Y	4–5Y	>5Y	Totals
Total Cash Outflows	−62	−46	−41	−11	−16	−11	−49	−236
Deposits	−60	−40	−40	−10	−15	−10	−40	−215
Own debt issues	−2	−6	−1	−1	−1	−1	−9	−21
Total Counterbalancing Capacity	0	0	0	0	0	0	0	0
Gap	**−12**	**−21**	**−26**	**4**	**9**	**14**	**61**	**29**
cum. Gap	−12	−33	−59	−55	−46	−32	29	

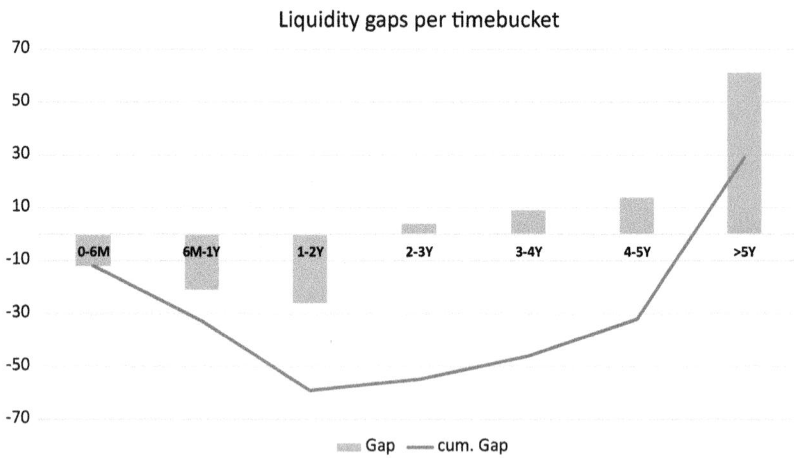

Figure 6.1 Liquidity gaps

EUR swap curve per 31.12.2019 as a proxy for the risk-free interest rate in Table 6.2.

Table 6.2 EUR swap rates per 31.12.2019

currency	tenor	swap rate
EUR	M06	−0,4075%
EUR	Y01	−0,3862%
EUR	Y02	−0,3634%
EUR	Y03	−0,3133%
EUR	Y04	−0,2615%
EUR	Y05	−0,2066%
EUR	Y07	−0,0750%
EUR	Y10	0,1272%

Austrian sovereign CDS spread history for various tenors as a proxy for the bank specific credit spread as depicted in Figure 6.2 (original data was scaled by factor 10).

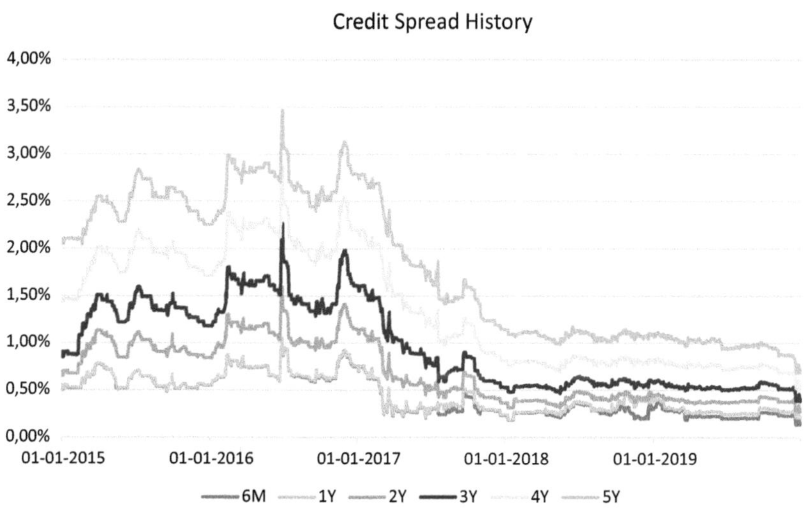

Figure 6.2 Credit spread history

6.2 R: YUIMA Package

YUIMA is a freely available R package and the name of the project of its origination. It is meant to provide a comprehensive environment for the simulation and inference for stochastic processes based on the R language.[1]

YUIMA package is used to estimate the parameters and run simulations of the jump-diffusion process mentioned in previous sections.

6.3 Estimating CIR Parameters

YUIMA package provides the function "qmle" for the quasi-maximum likelihood estimation of jump-diffusion processes.

The parameters are only estimated for Equation 5.1, thus excluding the jump-component, as a consequence of too rare occurrences of rating downgrades in the credit spread data to produce plausible estimates.

For the 6M spread the function provides the parameter estimates in Table 6.3.

Table 6.3 CIR parameter estimates

	Estimate	Std. Error
sigma (σ)	0.061687353	0.001191699
kappa (κ)	1.000130824	0.915878501
theta (θ)	0.004462487	0.001831374

The standard error for kappa, which is the speed of mean reversion, is significantly high. A reason therefore is visible in Figure 6.2. The history does not show long run mean reversion.

6.3.1 Estimation of the Jump Intensity

The dataset does not allow for a reliable estimation of the jump parameters with YUIMA package, as mentioned before. There are no recommendations or show cases in the literature sources.

To avoid an arbitrarily chosen jump intensity the following approach is proposed (with input data from Table 6.4):

[1] Iacus/Yoshida (2018) p. 3

Table 6.4 S&P's average one-year global financial institution's transition matrix (1981–2019)[2]

from/to	AAA	AA	A	BBB	BB	B	CCC/C	D	NR
AAA	86.08%	8.71%	0.43%	0.21%	0.11%	0.00%	0.00%	0.00%	4.46%
AA	0.36%	87.10%	8.37%	0.34%	0.00%	0.00%	0.00%	0.02%	3.82%
A	0.02%	1.96%	**87.82%**	4.37%	0.20%	0.05%	0.01%	0.06%	5.50%
BBB	0.00%	0.23%	3.82%	84.80%	3.54%	0.41%	0.04%	0.26%	6.90%
BB	0.00%	0.08%	0.08%	5.48%	77.43%	4.87%	0.55%	0.66%	10.85%
B	0.00%	0.00%	0.04%	0.29%	6.59%	76.62%	3.02%	2.84%	10.60%
CCC/C	0.00%	0.00%	0.00%	0.00%	0.77%	18.25%	45.50%	16.45%	19.02%

Assuming that the Austrian bank in focus has an S&P rating of single A, the chance of a rating downgrade within the next year is 4.63%, which is the sum of transition probabilities to BBB, BB, B and CCC/C.

A migration into the non-rated category NR is presumed to be without impact. The possibility of transition to the default class D is not considered, as refinancing is entirely impossible in this situation.

Possible rating improvements are not incorporated in the model, as the jump component is restricted to reflect downside risk only. Technically it would be possible to mimic rating upgrade behavior of credit spreads by choosing a proper distribution F, as illustrated in Figure 5.2 on page 42.

The probability that the bank will not experience a downgrade within the next year is 95.37% (this percentage includes the special cases of migrating to D and NR).

Lambda is now set as such, that

$$P(N_t = 0) = 95.37\% \tag{6.1}$$

where Nt is the number of events (jumps) occurring until time t distributed $N_t \sim Ps(\lambda)$.

This lambda is found by plugging into the probability mass function from Equation 5.10

$$P(N_t = 0) = \frac{\lambda^0}{0!} * e^{-\lambda} = e^{-\lambda} = 95.37\% \tag{6.2}$$

[2] Standard & Poor's (2020) n.pag.

and rearranging to

$$\lambda = -\ln(95.37\%) \approx 0.04741 \tag{6.3}$$

The conclusion is that Equation 6.1 holds true for a jump intensity λ of 0.04741.

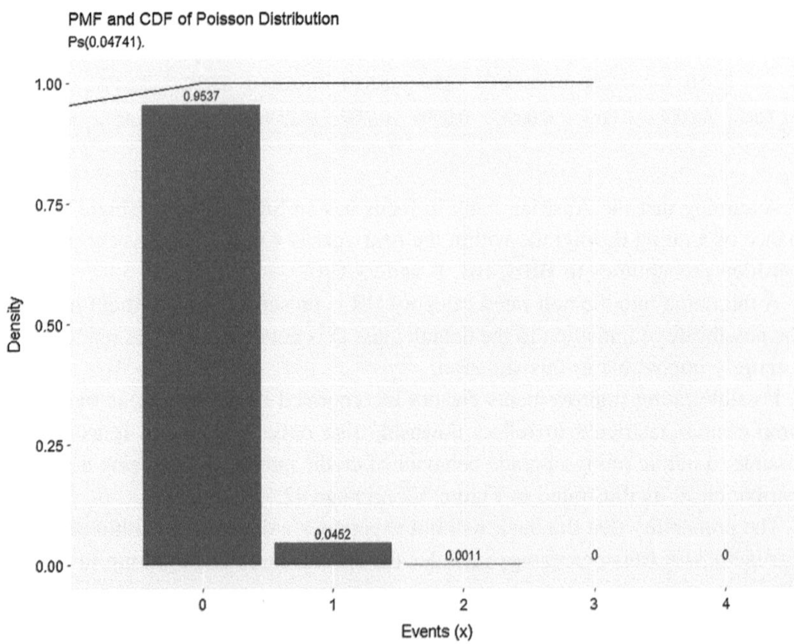

Figure 6.3 Probability mass function of *X ~ Ps(0.04741)*

The probability of experiencing not a single jump within a year (or 250 trading days) is 95.37% according to the probability mass function in Figure 6.3.

6.4 Simulating Credit Spread Development

The function "simulate" in YUIMA package allows the simulation of one single path of the specified jump-diffusion process. For simulating multiple paths, the function is required to run inside a loop that saves every path into an R object.

With the input parameters from Table 6.3 and a jump intensity ($\lambda = 0.04741$) derived from the institution's rating as well as the initial 6M credit spread level ($x_{init} = 0.00139$) from 31.12.2019 we can simulate the 5 example paths in Figure 6.4.

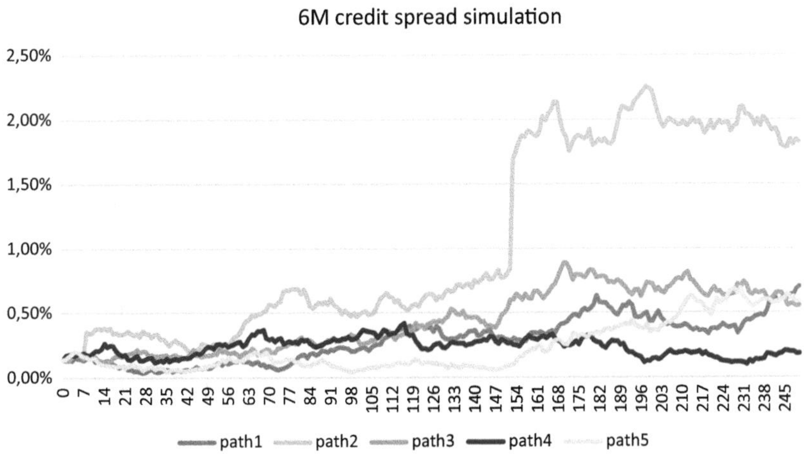

Figure 6.4 Simulation of the credit spread development

Path number 2 shows a jump on the 153rd trading day that can be interpreted as the impact of a rating downgrade on the credit spread.

Figure 6.5 depicts 10,000 simulated paths of the 6M credit spread over 250 trading days.

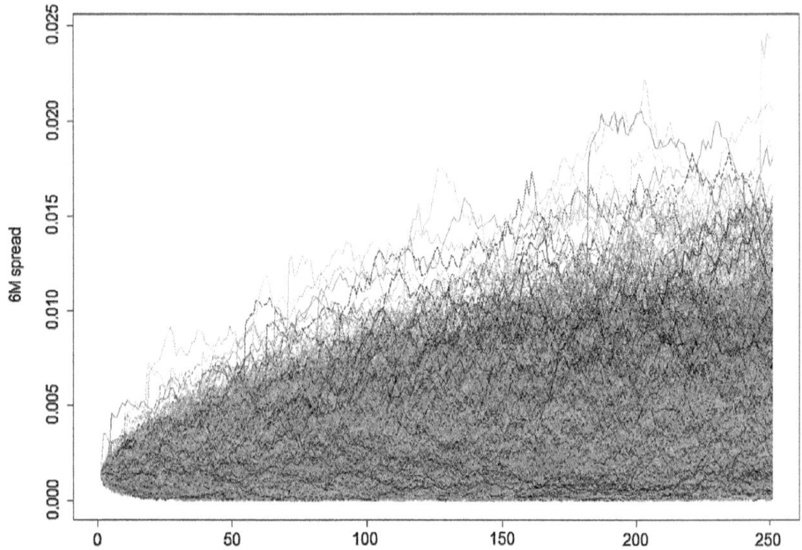

Figure 6.5 10,000 simulated paths of the 6M spread

After the simulation of 10,000 paths for the 6M credit spread the histogram of simulated spread end values is given in Figure 6.6.

The simulated distribution of end values shows the quantiles listed in Table 6.5.

6.5 Discounting Liquidity Gaps

As described in section 5.1 the chosen approach is to close all open liquidity positions on the bank's liquidity balance sheet in Table 6.1.

First the current funding costs are used to calculate PV_{base} with following discounting formula:

$$PV_{base(t)} = \frac{G_{(x,t)}}{(1 + r_{base(t)})^t} \tag{6.4}$$

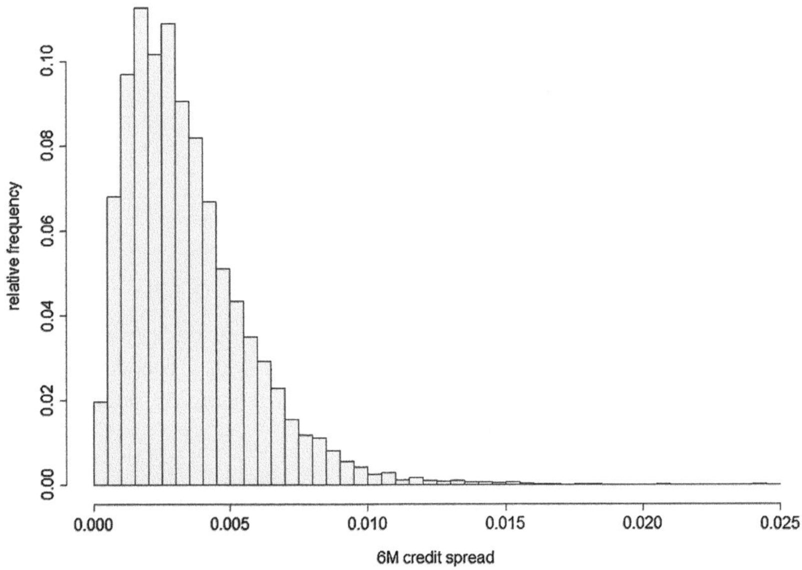

Figure 6.6 Histogram of simulated spread end points at $t = 250$

Table 6.5 Quantiles of the simulated distribution

$Q_{(p)}$	6M spread
p = 90%	0.006382547
p = 95%	0.007692562
p = 99%	0.010763068
p = 99.9%	0.015417823

where:

$G_{(x,t)}$ is the liquidity gap with x as index and t as the projected position of the gap, which is the upper bound of the respective time bucket (except for the last one)
$r_{base(t)}$ is the current credit spread added on top of the swap rate i for the tenor t:

$$r_{base(t)} = i_{(t)} + s_{base(t)} \tag{6.5}$$

Then the simulated spreads are used to calculate PV_{sim}:

$$PV_{sim(t)} = \frac{G_{(x,t)}}{(1 + r_{sim(t)})^t} \tag{6.6}$$

where:

$$r_{sim(t)} = i_{(t)} + s_{sim(t)} \tag{6.7}$$

As $s_{sim(t)}$ the 99.9%-quantile of the simulated distribution of credit spreads from Table 6.5 is used. The underlying assumption is that with a confidence level of 99.9% the credit spread does not exceed $s_{sim(t)}$ within 250 trading days (Figure 6.7).

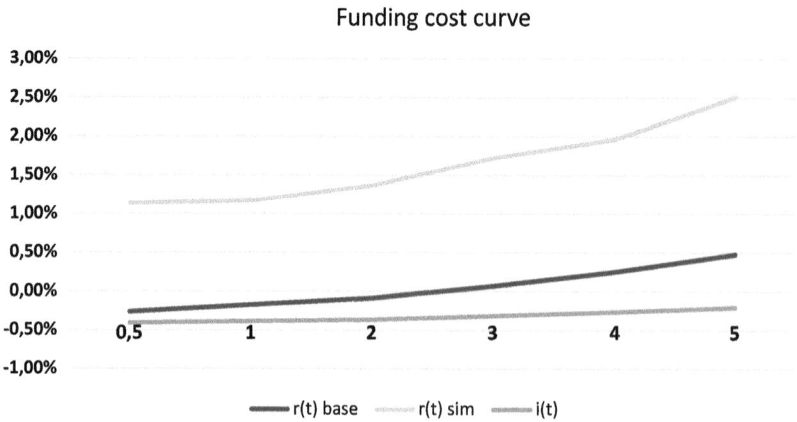

Figure 6.7 Funding costs in base and simulated scenario

The impact of the simulated change in refinancing costs on economic capital and respectively the risk-bearing capacity is given by Equation 6.8:

$$\Delta EC = \sum_{x=1}^{n} PV_{sim(x,t)} - \sum_{x=1}^{n} PV_{base(x,t)} \tag{6.8}$$

Table 6.6 shows the application of the described steps on the liquidity gaps of the balance sheet example.

The positive gap $G_{(6,5)} = 14$ means that in the time bucket 4–5Y more assets than liabilities are maturing. This leaves 14 units worth of assets without refinancing with a matching term liability. To close this gap the bank can issue a (hypothetical) zero coupon bond that creates an outflow of 14 units in this time bucket leading to the closure of the gap $G_{(6,5)}$.

The idea behind comparing $PV_{base(6,5)} = 13.67$ and $PV_{sim(6,5)} = 12.37$ is that issuing a (hypothetical) bond can create an immediate inflow of 13.67 in the base case, but only 12.37 in the simulated case. The difference are the increased funding costs for the bank with the simulated widening of credit spreads.

The negative gap $G_{(3,2)} = -26$ shows that in the time bucket 1–2Y more liabilities than assets are maturing. The bank must invest in a matching term asset that creates an inflow of 26 units in time bucket 1–2Y to close the gap.

In the chosen approach the asset investment is assumed to yield the same rates as the (hypothetical) bond issuance costs. Assets and liabilities are affected by the increased liquidity costs to the same extent, as mentioned in section 5.1. This is criticized in Enthofer/Haas (2018).[3]

The calculation of the case for the Austrian bank on reporting date 31.12.2019 results in a reduction of risk-bearing capacity of $\Delta EC = -6.65$. This is the maximum loss of present value resulting from structural liquidity risk over 250 trading days at a confidence level of 99.9%.

6.5.1 Reduced Extent of Maturity Transformation

Changing the liquidity balance sheet structure towards a lower extent of maturity transformation must result in a lower ΔEC (gap structure shown in Figure 6.8).

[3] Enthofer/Haas (2018) p. 926.

Table 6.6 Calculation of the impact on economic capital ΔEC

time bucket	x	t	G(x,t)	i(t)	s(t) base	s(t) sim	r(t) base	r(t) sim	PV(t) base	PV(t) sim	ΔPV(t)	ΔEC
0–6M	1	0.5	−12	−0.41%	0.14%	1.54%	−0.27%	1.13%	−12.02	−11.93	0.08	
6M–1Y	2	1	−21	−0.39%	0.21%	1.56%	−0.18%	1.17%	−21.04	−20.76	0.28	
1–2Y	3	2	−26	−0.36%	0.28%	1.73%	−0.09%	1.37%	−26.04	−25.30	0.74	
2–3Y	4	3	4	−0.31%	0.38%	2.04%	0.07%	1.72%	3.99	3.80	−0.19	
3–4Y	5	4	9	−0.26%	0.52%	2.22%	0.25%	1.96%	8.91	8.33	−0.58	
4–5Y	6	5	14	−0.21%	0.68%	2.72%	0.48%	2.51%	13.67	12.37	−1.30	
>5Y	7	5	61	−0.21%	0.68%	2.72%	0.48%	2.51%	59.57	53.89	−5.68	
									27.04	**20.39**	**−6.65**	**−6.65**

Table 6.7 Liquidity balance sheet with a lower extent of maturity transformation

	0–6M	6M–1Y	1–2Y	2–3Y	3–4Y	4–5Y	>5Y	Totals
Total Cash Inflows	50	25	15	15	25	25	110	265
Cash	15	0	0	0	0	0	0	15
Loans	30	20	10	10	20	20	100	210
Securities	5	5	5	5	5	5	10	40
Total Cash Outflows	−42	−36	−31	−21	−21	−21	−64	−236
Deposits	−40	−30	−30	−20	−20	−20	−55	−215
Own debt issues	−2	−6	−1	−1	−1	−1	−9	−21
Total Counterbalancing Capacity	0	0	0	0	0	0	0	0
Gap	**8**	**−11**	**−16**	**−6**	**4**	**4**	**46**	**29**
cum. Gap	8	−3	−19	−25	−21	−17	29	

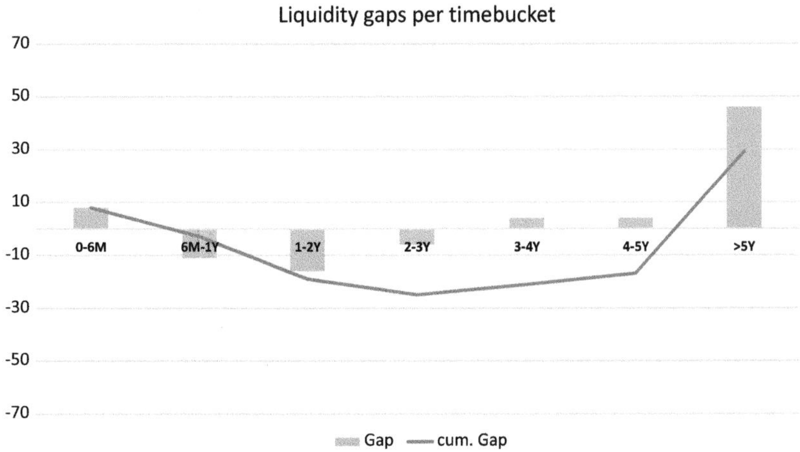

Figure 6.8 Gaps resulting from the liquidity balance sheet in Table 6.7

In Table 6.7 the average maturity of deposits has changed compared to Table 6.1 in the initial example. The amount of sight and short-term deposits is reduced, whereas the amount of longer-term deposits increased. Total amounts remain unchanged.

Table 6.8 Calculation of ΔEC with a lower extent of maturity transformation

time bucket	x	t	G(x,t)	i(t)	s(t) base	s(t) sim	r(t) base	r(t) sim	PV(t) base	PV(t) sim	ΔPV(t)	ΔEC
0–6M	1	0.5	8	−0.41%	0.14%	1.54%	−0.27%	1.13%	8.01	7.96	−0.06	
6M–1Y	2	1	−11	−0.39%	0.21%	1.56%	−0.18%	1.17%	−11.02	−10.87	0.15	
1–2Y	3	2	−16	−0.36%	0.28%	1.73%	−0.09%	1.37%	−16.03	−15.57	0.46	
2–3Y	4	3	−6	−0.31%	0.38%	2.04%	0.07%	1.72%	−5.99	−5.70	0.29	
3–4Y	5	4	4	−0.26%	0.52%	2.22%	0.25%	1.96%	3.96	3.70	−0.26	
4–5Y	6	5	4	−0.21%	0.68%	2.72%	0.48%	2.51%	3.91	3.53	−0.37	
>5Y	7	5	46	−0.21%	0.68%	2.72%	0.48%	2.51%	44.92	40.64	−4.28	
									27.76	**23.68**	**−4.08**	**−4.08**

A higher amount of assets can be matched with a deposit of the same maturity. Hence Table 6.7 shows a lower extent of maturity transformation compared to Table 6.1 and must show lower structural liquidity risk quantified by ΔEC.

The proposed model shows a lower impact on economic capital in Table 6.8 and can prove that it correctly indicates a lower structural liquidity risk in the liquidity balance sheet in Table 6.7 compared to the initial one in Table 6.1.

6.5.2 Liquidity Balance Sheet without Structural Liquidity Risk

A balance sheet without any open liquidity gaps would not be subject to structural liquidity risk. But there are also other hypothetical gap structures that would not show any structural liquidity risk from the computation of ΔEC.

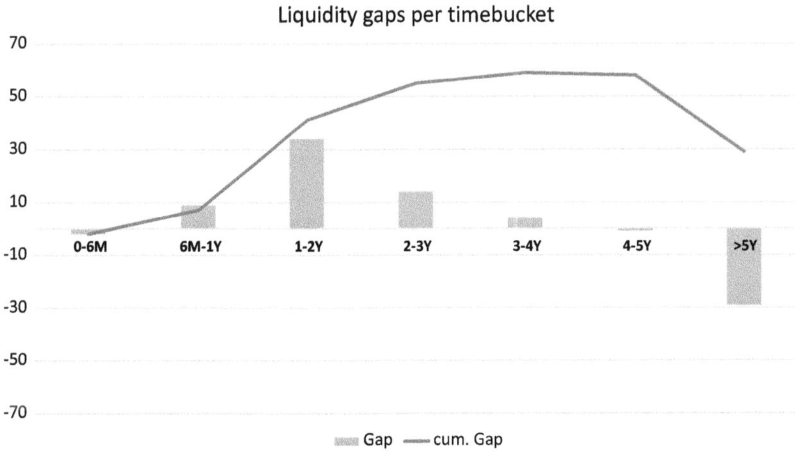

Figure 6.9 Gap structure without risk measured by ΔEC

Table 6.9 Liquidity balance sheet with very low average asset maturity

	0–6M	6M–1Y	1–2Y	2–3Y	3–4Y	4–5Y	>5Y	Totals
Total Cash Inflows	60	55	75	25	20	10	20	265
Cash	15	0	0	0	0	0	0	15
Loans	40	50	70	20	15	5	10	210
Securities	5	5	5	5	5	5	10	40
Total Cash Outflows	−62	−46	−41	−11	−16	−11	−49	−236
Deposits	−60	−40	−40	−10	−15	−10	−40	−215
Own debt issues	−2	−6	−1	−1	−1	−1	−9	−21
Total Counterbalancing Capacity	0	0	0	0	0	0	0	0
Gap	**−2**	**9**	**34**	**14**	**4**	**−1**	**−29**	**29**
cum. Gap	−2	7	41	55	59	58	29	

The structure of outflows in Table 6.9 is the same as in the initial Table 6.1, but the average remaining maturity of loans was drastically decreased by shifting repayments towards the earlier time buckets (Table 6.10).

For a gap structure as illustrated in Figure 6.9 the proposed model would show an increase in present value resulting from higher refinancing costs.

The reason for this output is already described on page 52. The negative gap $G_{(7,5)} = -29$ in the last time bucket is assumed to be closed by investing in an asset that yields the simulated refinancing costs. This creates a substantial positive contribution.

The intention is to measure downside risk and a positive ΔEC would indicate an improved risk-bearing capacity or a gain of economic capital. Therefore Equation 6.8 is modified to:

$$\Delta EC = \min(\sum_{x=1}^{n} PV_{sim(x,t)} - \sum_{x=1}^{n} PV_{base(x,t)}, 0) \tag{6.9}$$

Table 6.10 Calculation of ΔEC with very low average asset maturity

time bucket	x	t	G(x,t)	i(t)	s(t) base	s(t) sim	r(t) base	r(t) sim	PV(t) base	PV(t) sim	ΔPV(t)	ΔEC
0–6M	1	0.5	−2	−0.41%	0.14%	1.54%	−0.27%	1.13%	−2.00	−1.99	0.01	
6M–1Y	2	1	9	−0.39%	0.21%	1.56%	−0.18%	1.17%	9.02	8.90	−0.12	
1–2Y	3	2	34	−0.36%	0.28%	1.73%	−0.09%	1.37%	34.06	33.09	−0.97	
2–3Y	4	3	14	−0.31%	0.38%	2.04%	0.07%	1.72%	13.97	13.30	−0.67	
3–4Y	5	4	4	−0.26%	0.52%	2.22%	0.25%	1.96%	3.96	3.70	−0.26	
4–5Y	6	5	−1	−0.21%	0.68%	2.72%	0.48%	2.51%	−0.98	−0.88	0.09	
>5Y	7	5	−29	−0.21%	0.68%	2.72%	0.48%	2.51%	−28.32	−25.62	2.70	
									29.71	**30.50**	**0.79**	**0.00**

7 Conclusion

The proposed model has the capacity to provide an answer to the research question. The model's output is interpreted as the maximum loss in present value over 250 trading days at a confidence level of 99.9% resulting from structural liquidity risk.

7.1 Potential Improvements

The quality of this quantification is subject to discussion. The model is kept simple for a straightforward representation within this thesis, but several improvements and modifications are necessary for the potential use in liquidity risk management practice:

The quality and granularity of the underlying liquidity balance sheet is key. Higher granularity requires more time buckets, especially towards the long end of the maturity spectrum. The gaps of time buckets in the distant future create the biggest impact when discounting them with the differing refinancing costs.

The history of institution specific CDS spreads, if available, must be assessed, as a CIR process does not necessarily provide the best fit.

The derivation of the jump intensity should be based on more institution specific information, as the S&P global average one-year transition matrix of financial institutions covers a very broad pool of debtors.

The estimation of the distribution of jump sizes must be refined. Case studies of observed rating downgrades of Austrian or European banks can provide a basis for the estimation of expected jump size when a downgrade occurs.

C. Wieser, *Quantification of Structural Liquidity Risk in Banks*, BestMasters, https://doi.org/10.1007/978-3-658-39593-3_7

7.2 Assumptions and Weaknesses

A significant impact on the model output emerges from the assumption in Section 5.1 to close all open liquidity positions:

It implicitly creates a situation, in which it is possible for the bank to invest in assets that yield the stressed refinancing costs. This is not a realistic assumption. Enthofer/Haas (2018) also describes the option to close open asset-forward-gaps, meaning positive cumulative gaps. However, the example that is provided is not perfectly clear, adopts different implicit assumptions and lacks detailed explanation.

Different terms for the closing of negative gaps are worth to be investigated.

Another questionable assumption is the use of the swap rate including the credit spread add-on as funding cost curve. The credit spread is an important price factor in interbank, money and capital markets, hence only for wholesale funding. But financial institutions also rely on retail deposits in their funding mix. This characteristic creates the potential of an extension of the proposed model to reflect such a funding mix.

The assumptions for the credit spread behaviour are the following:

- Credit spread can be modelled with CIR process and possible rating downgrades can be incorporated by a jump component
    - o Constant long-run mean reversion
    - o Non-negative credit spreads
- Assumptions within the jump component
    - o Only positive jumps
    - o Occurrence of jump event is Poisson distributed
    - Constant intensity
        - Markov property for rating transitions
    - o Known jump size distribution
- Credit spread is uncorrelated with change in general level of interest rates

A weakness of the model is that the long-run mean is not adjusted when a rating downgrade occurs. Unfortunately, YUIMA package lacks the possibility to adjust the long-run mean inside a path simulation. But the impact in the calculated case is limited, as the speed of mean reversion was estimated to a weak (or slow) level in the utilized CDS spread histories.

The constant jump intensity may be criticized for implicitly assuming the Markov property. It is not possible to integrate the assumption, that a previously downgraded bank has a higher probability of further rating downgrades.

An additional shortcoming is that an independent process is estimated for each of the spread tenors. No correlation between the tenors of the CDS spreads is incorporated.

In conclusion, the proposed model provides the basis to build a more sophisticated model for the quantification of structural liquidity risk by incorporating the improvements listed in Section 7.1 and mitigation of weaknesses discussed in Section 7.2.

A potential for extension of this thesis and conduction of further research is to test different approaches for stressing the funding costs and different concepts for the closing of open liquidity positions.

References

Alt, R. (2010): Statistik: Eine Einführung für Wirtschaftswissenschaftler, Vienna: Linde Verlag

Arvanitis, A., et al. (1999): Modelling Credit Spread Behaviour, retrieved from: http://laurent.jeanpaul.free.fr/Credit_Spread_Modelling_ICBI_29_09_99_Paris.pdf, accessed on 31.07.2020

Austrian Financial Market Authority (2020): Glossary Entries: ICAAP, retrieved from: https://www.fma.gv.at/en/glossary/internal-capital-adequacy-assessment-process-icaap/, accessed on 31.07.2020

Barfield, R., et al. (2011): Practitioner's Guide to Basel III and Beyond, n.p.: Sweet & Maxwell

Bartetzky, P., et al. (2008): Handbuch Liquiditätsrisiko: Identifikation, Messung und Steuerung, Stuttgart: Schäffer Poeschel

Basel Committee on Banking Supervision (2005): An Explanatory Note on the Basel II IRB Risk Weight Functions, Basel: Bank for International Settlements

Basel Committee on Banking Supervision (2008): Principles for Sound Liquidity Risk Management and Supervision, Basel: Bank for International Settlements

Basel Committee on Banking Supervision (2013): Basel III: The Liquidity Coverage Ratio and liquidity risk monitoring tools, Basel: Bank for International Settlements

Basel Committee on Banking Supervision (2013): Monitoring tools for intraday liquidity management, Basel: Bank for International Settlements

Basel Committee on Banking Supervision (2014): Basel III: the net stable funding ratio, Basel: Bank for International Settlements

Castagna, A. / Fede, F. (2013): Measuring and Managing Liquidity Risk, Chichester: John Wiley & Sons

Deutsche Bundesbank (2008): Monthly Report September 2008, retrieved from: https://www.bundesbank.de/resource/blob/706910/a3600598dd44b61e37c20c80375b042f/mL/2008-09-monthly-report-data.pdf, accessed on 26.08.2020

Duttweiler, R. (2009): Managing Liquidity in Banks: A Top Down Approach, Chichester: John Wiley & Sons

Enthofer, H. / Haas, P. (2018): Asset Liability Management / Total Bank Management: Handbook & Practitioner‘s Manual, 2nd ed., Vienna: Linde Verlag

C. Wieser, *Quantification of Structural Liquidity Risk in Banks*, BestMasters, https://doi.org/10.1007/978-3-658-39593-3

European Banking Authority (2014): EBA FINAL draft implementing technical standards on additional liquidity monitoring metrics under Article 415(3)(b) of Regulation (EU) No 575/2013

Fiedler, R. (2011): Liquidity Modelling, London: Incisive Media

Hull, J. (2018): Options, Futures, and Other Derivatives, 9th ed., global ed., Essex: Pearson

Iacus, S. / Yoshida, N. (2018): Simulation and Inference for Stochastic Processes with YUIMA: A Comprehensive R Framework for SDEs and other Stochastic Processes, n.p.: Springer

Jorion, P. (2011): Financial Risk Manager Handbook, 6th ed., Hoboken: John Wiley & Sons

Matz, L., et. al. (2007): Liquidity Risk Measurement and Management: A practitioner's guide to global best practices, Singapore: John Wiley & Sons

Porteous, B. / Tapadar, P. (2006): Economic Capital and Financial Risk Management for Financial Services Firms and Conglomerates, New York: Palgrave Macmillan

Ross, S. (1996): Stochastic Processes, 2nd ed., Hoboken: John Wiley & Sons

Ruozi, R. / Ferrari, P. (2013): Liquidity Risk Management in Banks: Economic and Regulatory Issues, Berlin: Springer

Schierenbeck, H., et al. (2008): Ertragsorientiertes Bankmanagement: Band 2: Risiko-Controlling und integrierte Rendite-/Risikosteuerung, 9th ed., Wiesbaden: Gabler / GWV Fachverlage GmbH

Schmaltz, C. (2009): A Quantitative Liquidity Model for Banks, 1st ed., Wiesbaden: Gabler / GWV Fachverlage GmbH

Schultz, G., (2016): Investing in Mortgage-Backed and Asset-Backed Securities, Hoboken: John Wiley & Sons

Standard & Poor's (2020): Default, Transition, and Recovery: 2019 Annual Global Corporate Default And Rating Transition Study, retrieved from: https://www.spglobal.com/ratings/en/research/articles/200429-default-transition-and-recovery-2019-annual-global-corporate-default-and-rating-transition-study-11444862, accessed on 26.08.2020

Thonabauer, G. / Nösslinger, B. (2006): Guidelines on Bank-Wide Risk Management: Internal Capital Adequacy Assessment Process, Vienna: Oesterreichische Nationalbank (OeNB) and Austrian Financial Market Authority (FMA)

Venkat, S. / Baird, S. (2016): Liquidity Risk Management: A Practitioner's Perspective, Hoboken: John Wiley & Sons

MIX
Papier aus verantwortungsvollen Quellen
Paper from responsible sources
FSC® C105338

If you have any concerns about our products,
you can contact us on
ProductSafety@springernature.com

In case Publisher is established outside the EU,
the EU authorized representative is:
Springer Nature Customer Service Center GmbH
Europaplatz 3, 69115 Heidelberg, Germany

Printed by Libri Plureos GmbH
in Hamburg, Germany